Little Fish Big Pond

Little Fish Big Pond

John A. Smith

Writers Club Press
New York Lincoln Shanghai

Little Fish Big Pond

Writers Club Press
an imprint of iUniverse, Inc.

For information address:
iUniverse, Inc.
2021 Pine Lake Road, Suite 100
Lincoln, NE 68512
www.iuniverse.com

ISBN: 0-595-26361-5

Printed in the United States of America

"*What keeps hearts' from falseness in this flat region is that there is nowhere to hide and Plenty of room for vision. Only sound needs echo and dreads it's lack, a glance is accustomed to no glance back.*"

—Joseph Brodsky

"*Sæll er hinn er hranna hádýra vel stýrir (tíd erumk vitnis váda víngerd) unir sínu.*"

"*(Happy is that steerer of the tall animal of the waves (ship) who is well content with his lot. I Am practised in the Wolf's danger (Odin's) and wine-making (poetry-composing).*"

—Ref (Hofgarda-Ref) Gestsson

Contents

Several people (well, ok, a few people) have told me that they have enjoyed reading my articles and sharing the view with me from the deck of the Mermaid when a story of mine has appeared in a 'free' Caribbean sailor's magazine. These people will be familiar with a portion of the writing contained within this slim volume. For your support I say thank-you. Many more others however will have never read any of my attempts at literary coherency but for one reason or another (maybe you like fish) you have purchased this book. To you I dedicate it, for you are truly of the brave and hardy and bold sort and probably a bit wealthier than many of my cruising peers who will borrow a copy if they ever read it at all! My original title choice was to use one of the titles of my previous unpublished books, 'Letters From Sinking Ships' or 'Blue Water, Love and Hurricane', or 'It Have Fish in It and for a little while I played with a title based upon navigational lines of position, this however became rather tedious and was soon abandoned. Although the multiple dimensional metaphor of: wind, sea, water, intercepts, time, celestial spheres, continents, islands, ocean currents, foreign cultures and both local and non-local phenomenon made it appealing, it was unfortunately much too precise. Art is after all a compromise between an individuals psyche and certain objective principles of symmetry—something like a fishing trip aboard a sailing ship. We have a goal, we have a purpose and we tack around a bit but we find our way.

There is very little precise about this book and quite frankly some of it might make very little sense. Hopefully as sense departs we might grasp at entertainment for its' own sake and so I hope you find at least some of it entertaining. Going slowly aboard the Mermaid, represents an opportunity to fish a bit deeper. There are some fishing tales within.

There are in fact, 'fish' in it and like them is illusive and wanders a bit. Let that be my metaphor and my final word

ACKNOWLEDGEMENTS

Kappy for saying, "lets do it"; **Vianni** for the picnic table to sleep on and **Marius** for his blessing to sleep in the Swedish cemetery; **Delia and Hennis** for holding my mail for 20 years; **Bob Halsey** for no shoes; **Ken Klein** for Rocinante; **Tom Kelly** who paid my bail; The 'Select"few in St Barths; the **Wizards** and **Warlocks**, magic and peace; **Alistair** for the view from the mountaintop; **David Goldhill**, for the many miles and trustworthy hands; **Tom Migel,** who stayed when the mainsail blew out; **Jack T. Shepherd**, for the singing; **Scotty,** for not eating the cat; **Geoff Smith; John Volk; Connie and Larry Hambleton; Cuthbert Snagg M.B.E.; Pete Hudson,** 'cause I did not have to ask; **Augie Hollen,** who set the pace; **Deanna Flinn**; the **Millers** of **Symbio; Billy 'Bones' Pringle** (not the potato chip); **Digi-Soft** Computer Services in Hillsborough Carriacou, especially **Ms. Ronalyn Mitchell**.

I would like to pay special tribute to the seafaring people of the Grenadines with whom I have spent many years and shared many sea miles. The list is long, and includes **Capt. Zepherine Mclaren** of Windward, **Bertie Frazer** of Hillsborough and **Simeon Cudjoe** of Harvey Vale.

I salute you all.

"You say she ugly like ape, but my boat she beautiful, mon, swellin' in de deep sight of de hungry moon, not waverin' like woman ashore but movin' so straight she clear herself highway front of her, where sea all tarnish like silver and clouds hangin' so low dey like a wig; and when she swing and sway like Marilyn Monroe, all de fish lag behind like boys down East Bay Street way, followin' dis great big woman mystery movin' cross ocean with stars in she shrouds."

—Author unknown
{ Copied from a urinal wall in Barbados)

FOREWORD

"The Man, the Myth and the Madness" By **Capt. Fatty Goodlander**

The Mermaid of Carriacou is certainly the most famous 'island sloop' currently afloat in the Lesser Antilles. She's a special boat—a happy, blessed boat. Exactly why this particular beach-built vessel is so remarkable is difficult to say, yet easily felt once aboard her worn, rough-hewn decks. Her planks—her very bones!—seem to radiate a sense of freedom, contentment and rare possibility. She has a warm, friendly heart. To sail her is to love her since 1968, this has been true—and sailors through the Caribbean have sensed it. (Author's Note: True, some unfortunate people cannot feel the strong heartbeat of a good ship—nor feel the agony of her death throes upon a storm-tossed reef—but this article isn't written primarily for them. Instead it is written for…people who are willing to believe they can feel what they cannot measure. I personally am not sure there is a God in Heaven—yet I am certain the Mermaid of Carriacou has a soul. You may call me crazy; notice how unconcerned is my smile…) Mermaid of Carriacou was designed by British marine architect Sturling Burgess and built by Zepherine MacLaren at Windward, Carriacou, for American yachtsman and adventurer J. Lynton Rigg. She is 44 feet long with 13 feet of beam, and has a moderate draft. She is somewhat slab-sided—with sharp floors, extreme dead rise, and a graceful entry. She has a long, straight run aft. The design—especially when loaded with cargo and heeled by the Trades—is a sweet one. Rigg's idea was to build a fast "island sloop", and challenge all the local native boatbuilders to a rare race for a sizeable amount of money ($500 EC). Rigg's motivation was not to win, but to foster and rekindle the dying art of shipbuilding, which had been a flourishing business on the island until the early 1960's.

His simple yet clever plan was a success—a huge success. He had Mermaid built, and organized the Carriacou Regatta. His vessel easily walked away with 1st place, and all the local builders vowed: "Never again!" Numerous vessels were built to beat her—none did for many years. (It is rumored she won eight or nine Carriacou Regattas, before she started getting beat up by "cargo" boats with 2-inch deck beams: (hers are 8" x 8"!). Yet—in a sense—all of her varied challengers were winners. Shipbuilding on the tiny, dry unimportant island of Carriacou grew into a respected profession. Soon, Carriacou boats were sailing up and down the Lesser Antilles again, making a new name for themselves. People had work. People had pride. They used their boatbuilding skills and their knowledge of the sea to carve out a decent living on an otherwise dirt-poor rock.

An entire island got a new lease on life—and a new deserved reason for self-respect.

Perhaps that's why Mermaid of Carriacou has such a benign, welcoming spirit. Perhaps she carries some of the joyful pride of the many-hued people of Carriacou locked deep within her wooden heart. Of course, such a strange and wonderful vessel deserves an extraordinary owner/captain. Someone who is willing to devote their entire life to maintaining her rightful place in Caribbean history. Someone dumb enough to want to; smart enough to succeed. A wonderful, carefree fool of enormous proportions. Enter the notorious, the infamous, the scandalous, the improbable, the impossible, the outrageous Captain John Smith.

A famous boat with a rich past needs a strong legendary skipper—and "Mermaid of Carriacou" found one in Smith.

He is…John Smith is…hard to explain. He is a poet, a sailor, a writer, a rummy, a wood butcher, an optimist, a sailmaker, and explorer, a 10 cent philosopher, a madman, a Yankee Trader, an honest conman, a visionary, a genius, and a complete and utter fool.

John Smith is sorta like an Indiana Jones who got a little too twisted during the 1960's—and actually believed all that crap about peace, love, brotherhood, and the rights of man. In 1977, he heard that the Mermaid was for sale—cheap—because she was built without an engine, was too big to fish, and too small to carry freight. Smith rushed down-island, waving a fistful of Yankee Greenbacks, and proudly purchased her from the amazed and amused—sailors of Carriacou.

Lots of knowledgeable folks attempted to dissuade John from the purchase. One well-known USVI yachtsman said bluntly: "That boat ain't just leak'n, John—she's sinking! She ain't worth trying to bring back to life! Attempting to fix her up would be like putting perfume on a pig...!" Needless to say, John ignored the skeptics. He paid his money, took his chance, and has never regretted his decision. Thus, he gradually began to be known throughout the Caribbean as "De white mon wid de black mon's boat!

He's sailed from Maine to South America, and carried inter-island cargoes of fruits and trees and lumber and salt and anything/everything, which would pay. He oftimes charters his vessel for $50.00 per day per person. (When Smith says no frills—he means it! If you wanna glass of water, bring one.) Captain John Smith doesn't go by the rulebook. In fact, he ate his copy. Whatever. Just 'cause some idiot makes a rule, doesn't mean you should obey it, according to Smith. He's been repeatedly arrested for having too much fun, detained for not being serious enough, and nearly stomped to death by some violence-crazed Grenadian Gairy-goons who thought he was acting "far too free to be allowed to flee..." He still believes in weird, untrendy causes like truth, justice, and personal liberty, and often sails thousands of ocean miles while stopping in numerous foreign countries with only a few dollars in his pocket. As often as not, the pockets of his shorts rotted off months before. Why mend and repair what one doesn't have a need for? Dead Broke.

But—although Smith may have no money—he is not poor. He has his beloved boat, the limitless horizon as perpetual destination, and an ocean teeming with seafood. It is also almost impossible for John to walk into any sailor's bar from Nova Scotia to Brazil without having at least one person offering to buy him a drink. But mostly what Captain John Smith is—is irrepressible. He loves life so much—lives it so fully—has such a passion for each and every day, that just being enveloped in his aura of activity is fun. You can always get a 'contact high' from John. His mind is moving at a speed of a million nautical miles an hour and it touches down like lightning strikes of illumination.

Of course, John has a few loose screws—clearly. Once, he contacted this reporter to journalistically "cover" him as he discovered the Fountain of Youth which was guarded by a beautiful Brazilian Princess who possesses the Three Sacred Keys to the Three Sacred Gates...

He's the sort of guy who will solemnly advise you to save your empty toothpaste tubes. And, of course, you carefully follow his sage advice—but he'll forget to tell you why, and you might be a tad too embarrassed to ask. (Author's note to himself: Remember to ask John why to save those stupid toothpaste tubes which are rapidly filling up me medicine cabinet...) Just how John Smith came to be John Smith is harder to explain. He's originally from Connecticut. That's not much help. In the 60's he was involved with the training of dolphins in Key West. It dawned on him that his students had it far more together than their teachers. He arrived in the islands in the late 1960's. He soon purchased a 25-foot 'Seabird yawl', and began exploring. He's still at it. Sort of.

There were a couple of trimarans and a few odd monohulls between the Seabird yawl and his purchasing Mermaid of Carriacou. The trimaran, Water Rat, was struck by a tanker and nearly destroyed. Shipwrecked—he lived for awhile amid the tombstones in the Swedish Cemetery on St. Barths. The past is kinda fuzzy. Parts to it are (gratefully) lost forever. He headquartered out of St. Barths for awhile—back when that lovely island was a magic place filled with people of rare adventure. Everyone was so young, and free. Everyone would live forever. Tomorrow wouldn't/couldn't come. The wine and rum and champagne would never stop. Life was an endless, orgasmic party…Of course, it did come to an end—reality reared its ugly head—but John had scented the freedom of the sea for too long to ever consider returning to normalcy. Normal people seem to strike John as really really really weird. What motivates 'em? Why do they run so hard just to stay in place?

So John hung out with Jimmy Buffet, Foxy and Tess, Les Anderson, Bob Dylan, LouLou Magras, Neil Young, Mad Murphy, The Lov'n Spoonfuls, and other living legends who just happened to be Living the Life in Paradise.

He hauled vegetables, fished, and carried general cargo. A million and one money-making scheme were hatched—each was a "Wild and Crazy" adventure where—in the end—all concerned ended up with empty stomachs, pockets, and bank accounts. Oh, well, it was fun—a "Real Gas". It might have worked…but now there is a plan for carrying palm trees northward, and exchanging them for…On and on it went—and still goes.

John's entire life came to be somewhat of an art project in, and of, itself. The Mermaid of Carriacou has no engine, no electronics, no nutt'n. There have been books written about her (see Douglas Pyle's 'Clean Sweet Wind'); and books written aboard her Pictures of her have appeared in National Geographic, numerous marine and travel magazines and the island of Grenada even issued a 35-cent stamp in her honor. And the most amazing, glorious, astounding thing is that Smith and the Mermaid still exist. He actually sails around saying things like "My Boat is Slow but The Sea is Patient…". He appears to still believe that the pure force of Righteous Karma can carry you through.

There aren't many John Smith's around any more. Life in the electronic 90's have shut most of them down. They have "come to their senses!" They've "stopped fool'n around", and have begun to "make something of their lives!" Not John. No way! Life is still a "tire swing" to John, and he is indeed "still crazy after all these years…"

He's keeping The Dream alive. He has a wooden boat, which usually doesn't leak faster than he can bail it out. The wind is free. A bag of brown rice is still cheap. He doesn't have much else—but he's happy. And he certainly has no plans to stop.

Keep the faith, John!

KEY WEST, 1968. I JUMP OFF OF THE DOCK…INTO THE SOUTH

From New England, Key West is as far south as anyone can walk and, like a lot of the other "pilgrims" of the 1960's, I found myself on Mallory Dock—glad for the Oversea Highway and its bridges that lay behind me, but no less troubled by the total lack of bridges ahead. I would have to get into the water, get wet. It was a short jump from behind the bar at Captain Tony's Saloon and into the water at the U.S. Navy Dolphin Training Facility on Fleming Key. For several months, I spent half of my day in the water with bottlenose dolphins (Tursiops truncatus). The purpose of the project, was not the concern of we, (the handlers), or they (the handled). Mutual curiosity, and perhaps love of life and the sea, bonded the divers and the dolphins. At times it was difficult to tell who was the observed and who the observer.

Being in the water with a creature so attuned to its environment made me feel like a handicapped child surrounded by star athletes. The porpoises were patient with us: our breathing holes were on the wrong side of our heads and we were clumsy; but we still managed to enjoy each other's play and company.

Navy policy had schedules to meet, secret pacts to sign and progress to make. Dolphins and trainers were individual pawns in the kind of research project that science fiction movies are made of. The 'brass' and scientists who make policy were not looking for life forms in harmony; they wanted to see how well dolphins could be trained for military purposes. Congressional representatives, military 'brass', their wives, and the assembled multitudes of the rich and powerful; all gathered for a quarterly budget review demonstration of the animals' progress in training. The dolphins, (a young male and an older female named Dolly) decided in their fully-developed dolphin brains that making love was more important than responding to subsonic key-words. They would not perform their tasks. Mutinies like these reassured the trainers that "dolphin paradise" and human, expectations were—like the bridges on the Oversea Highway—options of route but not prerequisites of travel.

One morning, a wild bird flew over the armed marines and electric fences; and landed, in a training pen, to recover food scraps. I was in a neighboring pen with Dolly, (riding her dorsal or just scratching her belly) when a hail of stones startled us both. One of the project directors (of smaller brain and imagination than Dolly) was throwing bits of packed marl at the diving cormorant. The bird was hit in the head and fell to the water. Shocked and off balance, it swam in circles. To reach the bird, I had to climb a ladder, cross on a catwalk and climb down another ladder—not an easy task in full wet suit and after eight hours in the water. Meanwhile, 'Mr. Project Director' picked up a long pole as if to help...instead, he took a long, lazy swing (like Conan impersonating Arnold Palmer) and decapitated the bird! This was the man whose judgment and decisions defined my workplace and the lives of my charges, (Dolly and the rest). It was too much for me (silence has never been my greatest virtue) and I launched into a condemnation of the man and the attitude he just demonstrated. He explained that he had "humanely put an injured bird (by his rock) out of its misery". I consider myself "humane" for losing my job without ripping his face off!

I had become 'color-blind' to the difference between myself, the dolphins, the bird...and even this 'individual'. I was no longer willing to be employed by a system, which gained its strength, by emphasizing differences, rather than appreciating similarities. It was time to look for a lifestyle that had more in common with a dolphin's peace then with Human aggression.

FREEDOM AND RESPONSIBITY

In 1609 Huigh de Groot, a 21 year old lawyer hired by the Dutch East Company, published a document entitled: MARE LIBERIUM on the thesis that fish are the most important ocean resource, and that the sea should be free to everyone. This was an ancient argument worldwide but became a particularly important issue relative to the world spice trade, which until that time had been firmly in the hands of the Portuguese as a result of the Pope having divided the new world between Spain and Portugal. In 1501 Vasco de Gama had gained control of the Eastern Hemisphere by blockading the Red Sea and strangling the Venetian monopoly, then underselling them by 80%! The Dutch did not want to see a repeat of this in the Americas.

Indeed however there is another greater reality. The sea remains the common heritage of mankind, but as this century ends, it has also become the common responsibility of mankind. Most countries possessing a portion of coast line guarantee that any citizen may approach the high water mark for the purposes of fishing or navigation, and this has kindled a newer hopeful doctrine; that of the sea and its' shore as being within the "public trust" or even more magnanimously as part of our "Human Heritage." For a people who claw a living from the often harsh and frequently limited resources of small islands the free access to the sea, its' fishery and its' opportunities has been the lifeline which has sustained them. Nowhere is this more prevalent than in the southern islands of the Eastern Caribbean. Here the centuries old skills of the Scottish and New England shipwrights have been exercised and maintained to a degree almost unprecedented in developing countries.

These shipbuilding skills coupled with the freedoms and the equal treatment of seamen as freemen has allowed these people to develop a Maritime infrastructure and a spirit of independence rarely seen in ex-slave nations.

The 'trust' of the guild of these shipwrights who taught their skills in an exercise of that trust has allowed these small nations to evolve firm democratic principles and concepts while being relatively free of the stigma of being newly freed and relatively unskilled agricultural workers. These skills have evolved and manifested fishery practices which in the case of inshore whaling, are a direct outgrowth of this sharing of New England cultural tradition. I would be the last (as a Connecticut Yankee) to decry the whaling tradition as being unfounded in economic importance or social development and ultimately, cultural independence. Surely anyone can see the sense of maintaining the skills and boats, for in the event of economic collapse or a disaster to the tourist or agricultural sectors the sea and the creatures in it have traditionally been the 'life-raft' or hard times source of sustenance. A whale represents a lot of protein when shared within the framework of a small group of hunters, as is the case in Bequia.

This spring the I.W.C. (International Whaling Commission) meets in Grenada to discuss and vote upon the whaling issues of today, topics that include aboriginal fisheries, inshore whaling and killing techniques. Of the more than 40 member nations, none has the greater vote. Each nation has one (1) vote. Upon results of this voting will be determined the agenda for the whaling industry as we enter the new millennium. All this brings us full circle and back to "Mare Librium" and the relationships between equal partners. The entire population of the 4 voting nations in the Eastern Caribbean is approximately 1/2 million. The population of Japan is over 100 million and the population of China is over I billion, yet they each have the same voting power on these issues. If we complete one more full circle we return now to the principles of "Responsibility and Public Trust" and hopefully that concept of our "Human Heritage".

Invariably in all democratic institutions the desires of many people (49%) are put aside in order to fulfill the demands of the majority (51%), but we must broaden our view. We must consider this an issue, which will gain small rewards for the individual voting nations in the short run, while undermining the concept of our common heritage in the longer one. The spewing of pollutants, or the secret dumping of toxic waste and the massive toll of the Norwegian and Japanese whaling fleets in comparison to the very limited catch/quota of a small nation like St. Vincent seems absurd.

Yet today, hostility to policies that encourage environmental and wildlife protection, is clearly a more documented though less recognized a source of environmental harm. The 3 whales allotted to St. Vincent as part of their inshore whaling rights has little if any impact on the worlds' whale population. However, the VOTE of Dominica, St. Lucia, St. Vincent, and Grenada does potentially far greater harm by allowing the large fleets to operate. This continues the literal 'wholesale' slaughter of the worlds' whale herds in direct opposition to anti-whaling nations like New Zealand, the USA, Canada, France and Germany as well as most environmental organizations worldwide. It amounts almost to a state of schizophrenia: nations as voters are becoming alienated from our common heritage and our common responsibility by choosing platforms and leaders based upon the hierarchy of the contemporary economic power structure. This seems no surprise, after all the concept of inalienable human rights conferred on man by his creator grew out of the modern notion that man is the pinnacle of creation and lord of the world, and the ballot box becomes the common and in this case crude tool. It logically follows then, that in today's multicultural world the only truly reliable path to coexistence and cooperation must start at what lies infinitely deeper in human hearts and minds than political opinion, convictions, antipathies, and sympathies. It must be rooted to all living creatures, to nature, and to the universe.

There are some thinkers who claim that if the modern age began with the discovery and settlement of the Americas, it also ended there. This occurred in 1969 when an American stepped onto the surface of the moon and humanity saw itself as a small blue globe and a new age of humanity began. We call this new age post-modernism. Vaclev Havel has symbolized this as "a Bedouin mounted on a camel wearing traditional robes under which he is wearing jeans, with a transistor radio in his hands and a Coca-Cola advertisement on the camels' back." He meant not to ridicule or to shed any intellectual tears over the commercial expansion of the world which has destroyed so many cultures, but saw it as a symptom of this multicultural globe and as proof that 'something' is happening. And what has happened in the Caribbean is that the Government Ministers involved directly in the vote have chosen to ask for a 'secret ballot', recognizing that there is a substantial contradiction in advertising for Eco-tourism while allowing the hunting of whales and porpoises upon the worlds' oceans and along their shores.

While we ponder this, let us remember that Cetaceans evolved brains the size of ours 30 million years ago, ours reached its' present size only 100,00 years ago. Some particular adages come to mind: to place people and principles before personalities and reward, and to seek progress not perfection.

MY CHRISTMAS WINDS CHARTER

It is a beautiful clear and cool windy wintry morning here at Sandy Island, Carriacou. I moved here from Hillsborough to escape the election fever and noise that was gripping the country. Oft-times, though difficult, it is a good idea to put some distance between ones' self and the nearest rum shop. On an island if 13 square miles with over 135 such establishments it isn't easy!

I actually was on charter for awhile, well almost a charter. A gentleman I met some years before contacted me and said that as the result of a health problem he would have two or three months off from work and would like to go fishing and of course sailing. He particularly requested to fulfill a lifetime dream of his and spend at least one night offshore. Seeing no lights. Seeing no land. He knew my rates and my boat, and was in no rush. He sends me a 10% deposit and finally offered me about one third my normal rate! Now this is so little as to be almost an insult. Hiring my ship and fishing gear, my small boats and Me for a daily rate so close to "40 pieces of silver" that I told him Sundays would be free and we settled for $300 a week. I'd probably be better of working at a Wendy's with salad bar and medical benefits just automatically thrown into the deal, but that's not going sailing or fishing. Now he tells me he would like to go to Panama! This is about 1500 miles to leeward and he has no idea that to return to Carriacou I would have to go through the canal and around the world! Maybe visit relatives in Seattle! So we settle down to a week of short passages and inshore fishing while leisurely heading north.

The 'Christmas Winds', les "ventes-noel", commence and settle in at a constant 35-40 knots for a week. Fishing and even short hopping is a bit sloppy and very wet and with a wall of weather ahead of me that looks a teeny bit too much like very nasty, I seek anchorage in one of the Grenadines. As we entered the roadstead in Canouan the wind picked up even more creating miniature, waterspouts across the harbor, gusting 60 knots and boats are dragging everywhere, including the 90 foot ketch Irene which has run aground. I drop my main anchor, a #70 danforth with ½ inch chain while dousing my #4 jib and darn if it doesn't jam a rock and bend, then begin to drag. I quickly cut the lashings on 'Dr. Jekyl', my #250 storm anchor carried ready at the starboard cat-head. With this much metal on a strong rode Mermaid comes up snug, 100 yards to windward of the reef.

We waited four days hoping the weather would moderate, but it never really did, so we tie in the third reef and are off to Bequia to buy a new anchor. Bequia is very beautiful and very popular and a very crowded anchorage. The crew spent New Years Eve 1999 on deck on duty on fire watch. The threat of falling flares is very real. The New Year dawned clear and beautiful but still blowing 35 knots. My guest is unable to appreciate the beauty that abounds. Time is slipping away from him and he is getting more irritable every hour. Anyway, he insists that we must leave into the north for "St. Somewhere Else".

I explain that a week of this wind will have kicked up some mighty nasty seas in the island channels with nothing but open water for over 2000 miles. He is adamant and must get his moneys' worth. I put on my best sails (sailors always wear their good suit in bad weather) and we clear for Dominica. Within 10 hours we are out from the relative lee of St. Vincent, the seas are 12-16 footers and it is wet-wet-wet and quite spectacular, except that my guest is puking in the scuppers and complaining about my cooking, my home-made bread and my dog. After about 50 hours of this we can make out the vague shape of Dominica on the weather bow. We passed St. Lucia and Martinique well to leeward in the 2nd night. Now he demands to be taken to land.

I explain again that the earth is round, and mostly wet and that the nearest land is 2 miles under the keel. It will take at least 24 hours to reach the shelter of the Saints group and another half-day to reach Prince Rupert Bay. He is not happy with this, mentions legal action and believes that I have kidnapped him and am holding him hostage offshore to claim my daily silver!

The chap was getting a bit, you know what I mean, freaked-out: sleeping with a flare, an emotional wreck so…I wear ship while he is sulking in the cabin, Suddenly it is calmer and we are moving south, scudding down the faces of the seas at over nine knots! Carriacou is straight ahead and I try to explain rhumb lines and curved surfaces and horizon distances et cetera. I feel like I'm on the bench with Columbus arguing with the Inquisition.

I got the fella to the beach after spending just over 112 hours at sea on this particular jaunt. Not really a passage because we never really went anywhere. It was more like a kind of self-imposed initiation rite. Wild water, bitter seas, savage kingdoms and a bit of the oceanic food chain. We saw 3 different types of whale on this trip. These thoughts come so easily in hindsight

For 36 years he had dreamed of his first night at sea, but because he hurried, as was his right, he has grown alienated from his love and mistress, the sea, and taken sides with that ages old enemy the "clock". He harbors no desire to pursue his relationship with the open sea. At last word he was living on the beach addressing picture postcards of ideal dreamlike days to other people who also confuse "fussiness" with culture, a well worn tourist guide with experience, a GPS position with the terrain and financial resources with sophistication. To "take and keep the sea", means just that. You exercise your skills and take advantage of your privilege. As the carnival barker explains, you makes your choices and you takes your chances. Except for turning on the EPIRB and then paying the hugefines for setting off a false signal, there is no quick way back. The sea will cover your tracks faster than the birds ate

"Hansel and Gretels" popcorn. The difference is that we are adults and should know better.

So if you should decide to "take and keep" the sea for a few days or a few months, look in the mirror first, preferably naked and acknowledge what "poor forked worms" we all are, when caught standing devoid of money, power, access and lawyers. Mindful of life's uncertainties, ask yourself the question: are you a man, a woman, or a schmuck? You have to decide, and then, assume the responsibility that goes with choice "It is very easy to wake a sleeping person, but impossible to wake someone who pretends to be asleep."

THE SIMPLE LIFE

Not long ago while enjoying an 'eighth' or a 'gill' of rum with a flat coke and no ice in a small rum shop adjacent to an upscale restaurant, a tourist approached the bar and asked for a 'diet coke'. "None here" I said, "life is to short to diet." "I'd like to be as thin as you" he said, then immediately asked me, "What do you do for a living?" The fella did not ask me how I got by. He did not ask me if perhaps there might be a bit of a sacrifice required to live, what now while on vacation, to him appeared the "good life in paradise".

He wanted the advantages, the security and the accoutrements of his American lifestyle plus the joys of 'the simple life'. Perhaps he sat in a yoga position 8 hours a week and resolutely believed that (though he meditated with the TV on) he would as a result of his perseverance and questioning find a sort of spiritual enlightenment and perhaps an alternative to drinking diet beverages.

I have owned and lived aboard a homemade (rough, not crude) wooden sailing vessel of some 20 tons displacement some 24 years. Prior to this vessel I have owned 4 others and, except for living in the Swedish Cemetery in St. Barths when shipwrecked in 1975, I have been aboard since '1968. Fortunately for me, the Swedish Ambassador, a Creole-Swede with 14 children, none of them blonde, told the Gendarmes that I was in fact his bastard son, (Thanks Marius!) and as a shipwrecked mariner should be allowed to find refuge among the cold marble and Swedish names

I have never had an engine, a refrigerator or a marine toilet. I do not have boat insurance or life insurance. I do not own a car, have a drivers' license, own a house or any land. I do not have a bank balance because I never had a bank account. I do not have a TV, a VCR, a microwave, shower, Jacuzzi or for that matter running water. But I am very mobile and have frequently spent over 250 days a year engaged in my favorite activities of fishing or sailing. I have no major health problems (tap-tap wood) no ulcers, all my teeth and all my hair. I've got plenty of hair. I do drink occasionally to excess, but not frequently. I smoke about one pack of cigarettes a week and most of the time I am barefoot and except for shorts, shirts and hats, clothes are not very important. Right now mangoes, avocados and bananas are ripening and this morning at the government market I bought 8 avocados, 6 mangoes, 10 banana, 16 passion fruit and a dozen limes for less than $6 US. I regularly purchase fresh jack-fish for $1 US a pound. (I do have to clean and cook them myself.) I never tire of fresh vegetables, fruit and fish. I rarely eat meat, ice cream, go to restaurants or smoke Cuban cigars.

But, I did not take the time to explain all that to this particular tourist, he really did not want to hear it. So I told him I sold machine guns and drugs. He seemed relieved. His pre-conceptions and his prejudices proved well founded. He believed somehow that only by being 'immoral' or by tying myself to his particular work ethic could I exist as the free man standing in front of him.

I finished my flat drink while he and his friends drank white wine and enjoyed a 5-course meal before returning to their chartered yacht and perhaps a night-cap of diet coke. I'm sure that they slept well, knowing that in under 2 weeks they would return to the 'real world', but I don't think that they learned a thing about mine or where I've chosen to live.

Like many a 'conquistador' before them they carried their baggage and trappings, sought their own personal "El Dorado" and did not learn anything about where they were or the cultures that they encountered, while very effectively eroding them. That is why I like these 'of the track' islands of the Caribbean. Only by spending some of ones' lifetime here can one come to appreciate what is valuable and what is not. Most people have a pretty full schuedle. They are busy with "matters of consequence". They do not take the time to smell the flowers or learn much less ask the right questions or better yet—ask no questions at all.

A long time ago in an enchanted land that existed among the salt-water marshes along the southern coast of New England, in a place the native people called "connect-the-cut", there lived a young prince who declared the waters of his birth place his realm and was met with scorn from other young princes because he preferred his boat to their two or four wheeled carriages and because he preferred chasing the resident striped bass and the pelagic bluefish to chasing the young princesses in his village. Princesses were in residence the year round but the bluefish and menhaden run lasted only one month.

As time went by the young prince, like young men everywhere, decided the world deserved exploring and perhaps a bit of research into fishing in other places. Places that did not freeze solid in the winter. So the young man moved to the southernmost point in his vast country, reached only by crossing a series of ancient bridges that once supported a railway line. Once upon this magic island, with bridges behind it, the prince worked for the King training dolphins to perform tasks which he did not understand. He did however come to view the dolphins as noble creatures who gained his respect for their patience with the race of men and their exceptional skill as fisherman. But he could not communicate with these creatures, and he returned to the land of men the mythological fishermen of an island to the south where the famous writer and fisherman of his father's generation had written a beautiful story about an old man and the sea which had become world famous for beautiful simple honesty. And so these people from the long island to the south became his teachers, but he grew frustrated with the increased reliance upon internal combustion engines and longed for a place where he might use his skills as a seaman and fisherman and learn to sail. To harness the wind to tow his baits and thus the young prince became a King himself with the shadow of his sails providing him with a palace, his deck providing a throne and for a host the ever present seagulls, each representing the soul of a fisherman who had passed this way before His ship was built by the master shipwrights of the small island of Carriacou. Originally a bit of a white elephant, built as a racing sloop, too small to carry cargo and too big to fish in the traditional way. He combined the skills of his Blue Water ancestors in the north where water freezes with the skills he had learned on the magic island of the bridges behind it and set himself a task: to hunt the most strong and noble fishes of the deep ocean from a worthy blue water ship. to share this combination of skills and opportunity with a few select fishermen/sailors who would prefer to watch behind the ship at it's wake and the baits ratherthan seek a buoy or racing marker off the bow. In other words to go sailing, not be taken fora ride, go fishing and actually catch fish.

It is a wonderful thing to awaken on the deck at first light, cast off the mooring pennant and drift out of the anchorage to the smell of fresh coffee. Catch a small tuna or bonito for breakfast then to gybe around to hoist the mainsail on an outbound tack towards the hundred fathom ledge just 2 miles offshore. Rig the big baits, one long line on the surface and a deep bait on the down-rigger. Sipping coffee from under the permanent awning in a deck chair or on a mat on the deck. It is silent except for the swirl of the wake and the slight shiver in the luff of the big gaff mainsail, the boat is soon trimmed to self-steer.

The Captain and crew have gone away. They have gone sailing. They have gone fishing. One ship, two fishhooks, no trespass. Tasting the adventure. Sharing the responsibility. Having another cup of coffee. Join me if you'd like.

TIMES AIN'T NOW WHAT THEY USED TO BE-ST. THOMAS 1970

I had heard of and infrequently met people who had talked about doing it. I never met anyone who actually did it. Lately I'd felt like doing it—you know, getting away; changing my space. Not for just around the corner or across the country, or the far edge of vision…beyond the limits of sight. I had remained one of the waiting watchers haunched on the shore gambling with freedom; and hoping for more than the occasional glimpse at the freedom of living one's dream, in the sunshine.

Solar energy may or may not be suitable for application as an industrial power source, but to me seemed an absolute necessity. A lifetime of alternate, teasing, short-lived summers and eternal winters, served as due cause for flights of fancy, to points preferably between the Tropics of Cancer and Capricorn. I had taken to going on late-night runs or when possible, long swims to emulate a "Dolphin" peace, too work out the tears and fear, the love and the fury of a spirit trying to fly yet shackled to the shore. That state of physical exhaustion resolved, if only temporarily, my inner boilings. I found myself walking not with the rolling gait of a sailor but living in a condition of "parade-rest" and strangely angry.

I flew, with neither malice nor aforethought, to the U.S. Virgin Islands to commence (in the sun) a search for a more personable tomorrow. I had all the sun I wanted, cleaner water than I had ever seen, and a horizon which o'rfilled my expectations. The license plate of each car and truck I saw reminded me that this was an "American Paradise": but I was not yet afloat!

Out walking and hitching along the main, I was given a lift by a dude who laid some advice on me; he said, "Sit tight, stand fast, hang loose, let things come". I slept on the bar at "Fearless Fred's" in Yacht Haven, St. Thomas. Months later, I invested my $500, lots of credit and karma in the twenty-five foot, mahogany and oak, 'Seabird Yawl', which had just arrived from Hawaii, crewed by a foursome who were exhibiting the signs of long-term confinement: I had a ship!

My first voyage was a near disaster (one close and one actual collision, and a grounding), but the forty years of cruising momentum of my Rocinante (ex Kona) gracefully compensated for my lack of skill. To the salt-crusted eyes of veteran cruisers sipping morning beers, it may have even appeared as if I knew what I was doing. The next several months were spent becoming more familiar with the single-handed management of a sailing vessel at sea.

A semi-permanent base on the North side of Great St. James Island (where several 'cruisers' maintained a small shack and some gardens) became homeport. A rocky, cactus-covered isthmus protected us from overland visitations by persons anchored in Christmas Cove. An unmarked reef at the mouth of the bay restricted entry to sailors with local knowledge or 'a spirit of adventure' to match our own. The frequent sighting of naked people on the beach gave to us a degree of notoriety, and our quiet corner became known as "Bare-Ass Bay". (Streets, Guide to the Virgin Islands, 1970)

There was gardening to do, yogurt to make, bread to bake and, a couple of times a week, we set out on hunting expeditions to the wreck on windward shore of the island. We swam the half-mile along the coast. We were attempting survival as "creatures of the seashore". Clumsy, and barely amphibious, echoing perhaps the deep-sea calls of our cousins, the great-whales and dolphins, we found joy in hunting for our 'daily bread'.

Re-provisioning of staple foodstuffs became a monthly necessity. Coffee, milk, flour, kerosene, candles and, what the hell, maybe a beer or three. A new harmonica for Ben, who had put his on a string. Clothes, much less pockets, were infrequently worn, and not pausing to consider the consequences of his freedom, he jumped with it into the ocean. So I return to St. Thomas across the Sound of Pillsbury, and into the harbor of Red Hook to replenish our island larder.

Much too early the following morning my 'guests' were climbing over the canary-yellow bulwarks of their US Government-owned out-drive runabout. Stepping with shiny black shoes upon my deck, show-ing badges and brandishing guns, they searched the ship's shelves and drawers, books and binnacle; until someone found some 'Mary G Wanna' seeds in the bilge. With an "aha, we got ya" they read me my rights, then took them away. Handcuffs defied the supposed sanctity of ship. This sailor was caught with his pants down after a short night's sleep. These "hired guns of anyone's sons worth the salt of the hire" dragged the "lord of the house, master of the ship" onto the wharf and into the streets that any "man-jack" among us could have built; saying and mocking him saying, "show us yourself at that self's worst, that our guilt will not cast shadow in the cool, clear, sophoclean early morning light". On the spot I was arrested, handcuffed, cramped twixt and tweened, while trussed and spiritually tarred by only-that-morning-deputized agents of "Law 'n Order".

The morning 'round-up' amounted to five men, two women, a fifty-three foot Ketch, a twenty-five foot Yawl, two Houseboats, and a Hulk that had not touched water for ten years. The total seizure was less than one ounce of Marijuana. We all took a walk within the six-foot-thick walls of Fort Christian, and looked up at the blue sky through the iron bars and waving flags. I sat on a bench and rolled a cigarette and the Marshall warned of "false moves". Someone laughed and said: "He's a lousy shot". This is the zen of prisoner wishing he were an arrow of 'Samsara'. (Smoking my pipe and reading "Candide", Dr. Pangloss remarks that "this is the most perfect of all possible moments", though I hear no clicking of wind-whipped palms…Only the awareness of the silence of the same, as when the full moon's call tempts sailors ashore to share the fruits of rain-kissed earth.)

We were all immediately charged with "trafficking a controlled substance in US waters". Bail was set. There were no beds available in the prison so we were asked to "please return at nine sharp the next morning", to be re-jailed pending post of bond. The lawyer appointed by the court was about to leave on vacation, but promised he would be in touch in a "month or so". Ho-hum. When he returned…everyone had gone sailing! The fifty-three foot Ketch was lost, with all hands, South of St. Croix. Both Houseboats sank. The 'hulk' originally named the "Pinafore" became the 'Bottoms-Up' bar and restaurant at the present day Independent Boatyard.

Several years later in St. Maarten I sat aboard my rebuilt ketch-rigged Trimaran Undina. Saba and Statia were just a hint of what was over the horizon. I gave away what I considered some inefficient (and all too frequently ill-affected) machinery: a 4 hp outboard engine to a Dominican fruit-boat and an 18 hp. outboard engine to the one hundred-and-fifteen year old cruising Schooner the Klaraborg of Sweden. Once again involved in the many varied and provocative stimuli, which are such a part of the 'maintenance program' of this 'planet' my ship. More specifically…I pulled out the 'marine Head' (with its intricate, incomprehensible, and often awry array of pumps, valves, seacocks and other such nonsense) and painted a yellow-stripe around a bucket.

The crew was sworn-in and piped aboard: First mate Ira Epstein had sailed many a voyage, and 'Lady' Deborah sought passage. Tadpoles and tenderfeet are happy in small places, but a sailing vessel and her crew need a bit of 'sea-room'. In the morning we shot the gap, leaving Saba to Starboard and Statia to Port.

Sunrise of the fifth day and Bonaire lies fifteen miles to windward, on a steadily veering force-eight day. A quick evaluation of the situation (punctuated by a 45-knot gust) prompted a double ration of the ship's 'Grog' all around. We changed course, from a wet, Close-reach to an exhilarating sleigh-ride of a Run at fifteen knots, to round up in Westpunt Baai, Curacao at sunset while eating popcorn from paper bags. The crews' feet were itching to go ashore: but a hot meal and a good night's sleep took priority.

A cold beer in the morning, and a "howdy do" to Immigration who were sorry to say that "though they realized it was blowing a gale out-side, and oh yes, they had cars: it was a long drive and would we please sail to Willemstad?" I had been there before on Rocinante and didn't 'relish' the idea of tacking through the rotting vegetables and oil-slick, next to the bridge 'Swinging Emma'. We agreed to meet them halfway and get vessel and crew list to Piscadera Baai which of course was dead to windward. A 40-knot gust blew out the Mizzen sail…scuttling any plans of rendezvous or landfall again in Curacao. Aruba was eighty miles away and a reach. The working-jib managed to hold together until just off the windward southcoast, when it decided to pack it in and join the ranks of the recently retired Main and Mizzen. Time to call out "old reliable" (the hand sewn, three layer, number one canvas, bolt-roped Trys'l) as a Jib we scoot under the lee of the huge 'Exxon' refinery, the glow of which rendered invaluable-aid in reminding us of our proximity to that surf-and coral-rimmed shore.

Debbie, who was obviously "vexed by de whole ting", demanded to be taken ashore. I smiled and explained that this was "not a drill" but if she would like to swim, I'd throw her "in the direction of the beach".

We spent a windy evening on deck re-sewing the Working-Jib, and shifted the Trys'l to the Quarterdeck as a lateen-rigged Mizzen (a posi-tion worthy of the long service rendered). We were tired, and the light of dawn seemed only to increase the span of rough water between us and the shore. What we had presumed to be shorelights were in fact the riding-lights of half-a-dozen tankers, queuing to offload 'crude' in the roadstead that is Palm Bay. Countless Tacks later after a giant uphill slalom we were on twin 'hooks', feeling very mortal, yet very much alive.

Five minutes after we had anchored, the Deb appeared on deck, "packed and ready to go". She was held in Ira's protective custody while I contacted Immigration so that the ship and crew might 'enter' with an air of propriety commensurate to the experience of the voyage. The crew was pretty exhausted. Debbie hadn't known what to expect when she came aboard…She had never been to sea, and imagined the boat to be a sundrenched platform on which to lie, with her bikini top off, while riding to exotic ports to the South and West. Neither infrequently nor quietly did she express a desire for "the whole operation to sink" and thus end her agony. To Ira it had been "a damn good trip", and within a week heleft on the Schooner Lord Jim for San Francisco.

Single-handed again; with no sails, little food, no dollars…and hurricane "CARLA" thrashing around not far away. The fishing boat King offered to tow me into the mangroves where I could make repairs. Immigration officers visited me daily…I could stay two weeks. I received much help from local sailors and fishermen…and Social-welfare people who (in landsman jargon) explained the situation. I was given a one week extension. 'Water-Rat' cleared port and sailed eastward hoping to find a more hospitable anchorage…and thus found itself close-onto Cabo Bravo (or "Mad Point") on the Paraguana Peninsula in Northern Venezuela. If madness is a point, then I touched upon it wetted my feet ripped the bottom out of my starboard Ama nd sailed away. It was a near-shipwreck in breaking seas. My boat was holed, swept clean, but afloat. Aflight, so lightly as a Trimaran, yet leaking as a holed boat is ought. Pumping and bucketing, single-handing, clawing for searoom away from the coast…and then away from the bow of a rapidly approaching tanker. Half sinking, holding baresteerage…my first three flares failed. My fourth, when hand-thrown, hit the Starboard-bow of the biggest wall of darkness, noise and water I could imagine. I lit another flare and was lifted by the wave and dwarfed by the sound, as this mechanical behemoth of the sea neither stopped nor strayed; for with the wind in our teeth and the rocks at our backs even if I had been seen it was a foul night and the place was wrong. A ship is a ship and, as my responsibility was to my vessel, those on the bridge of the tanker were obliged to maintain their distance from the same "Mad Point".

Two days later I sailed my jury-rigged ketch, to Piscadera Baai, Curacao sold the boat that afternoon and woke the next day in the Venezuelan Andes, dizzy on the thin air and numb from the cold. Distilling time into wine and getting drunk on gospel. Hunched-down, dragging knuckles and ready to jump any fence rather than kill a poem with a moment of hesitation. Day-glow sailor, struggling to accentuate the simultaneous natures of his small ship and our small planet.

Aware of ecological and environmental values on a scale much broader than that of economic or party politics, refusing to compromise the beauty of a sailing ship's energy sources and the poetry of interaction. No reason to consult the future to know how I feel now. It's a state of mind, an attitude. I like to travel light and fast—like cavalry. I don't like internal-combustion engines. I'm intrigued yet frustrated by electronic equipment (to give it reality somehow tampers with mine). And adopting an American or European lifestyle places me at the mercy of those self same 'Corporations' my sense of values condemns. I prefer not to spend or 'consume' time. There is only one worthwhile sort of work: that of the imagination, and messing about with boats seems best able to couple the flight of a fanciful mind with a body of clay.

THE BEACHES OF HOME

I read one day how all the waters of my home town were safe for swimming. So I told myself that maybe I'm not supposed to be able to see my feet when I'm in water only up to my knees. I hear about 'Keypone' poison levels in bluefish; but I've been fishin' 'blues' for over forty years and because I'm doing the catching, killing and cleaning I feel better about eating them than I do about eating one of the twenty-billion or more McDonald's hamburgers.

Some of my fondest memories of Milford revolve around walking along the shore at low tide and diggin' an occasional steamer or razor clam. Well, now I'm told how that's "not allowed" as it's unhealthy. These animals of the tidal flats evolve from a life chain much longer than my human past, and they're simple, basic creatures. But it's okay for me to swim? Maybe with all these shark-scares the solution would be to post underwater warnings: "CAUTION…Eating humans may be hazardous to your health". If the sharks can see through the murk.

Humans are smart and adaptable; but are we using our intelligence to correct the pollutionproblem or are we just adapting to it?

It's kind of sad to hear that none of the oysters at the recent "Oyster Festival" were from local waters and that most of the oyster boats are now in museums. I wrote this letter with a Bic pen and when I shave I sometimes use Schick blades; but I'd rather be a hirsute barefoot mute, digging local clams and safely eating fresh-caught fish. Now and then a clean spot finds its way through the flotsam, detritus and murk.

THE TALL SHIP ROSE

I have divulged the shadowy secret of my New England "swamp-Yankee" heritage. Allow me therefore to fall back upon the accidental geography of my birth and provide an explanation for my interest or obsession with historic or replica craft among the tall-ship fleets of the world, which frequently appear as if out of an other time or era and anchor up among more pedestrian cruising fleets. Bequia St. Vincent, is not excluded in such occurrences for it was here that I first witnessed the spectacle of just such a vessel anchoring up on my port beam. A vessel such as the Rose entering a roadstead is hard to ignore or properly acknowledge.

I have been to Boston and seen "Old Ironsides", the USS Constitution (the oldest still-commissioned vessel in the US Navy) but that was long before its refit in an attempt to get the old wagon sailing for the turn of the millennium. But apart from reversing itself port/starboard at the Boston Pier where it lies, it has remained rather stationary.

The 'replica' was built to the original lines of HMS Rose which played a very important role in the American Revolution. The original Rose was a typical 32-gunner of the period, about 125 feet in length with a 35-foot beam and 12-foot draft. Armed with 18 pound cannon, 12 pounders and 9 pounders, and of a class which included the HMS Vestal, Minerva, Milford, and Flora, she represented a major "interference" of Yankee smuggling and blockade running when she arrived on station off of Rhode Island in 1775. The Yankees had been making a damned nuisance of themselves for several years now. In 1772 the British revenue cutter Gaspee, aground off of Narragansett, was seized and burned by Rhode Islanders led by Abraham Whipple. The British immediately threatened to hang Capt. Whipple who advised the British "To catch a man before you hang him". Then in December of 1773 the rebels, dressed as Mohawk Indians, tipped the tea off of several British ships into Boston Harbor, and in 1775 the Rhode Islanders led by none other than the indomitable Capt. Whipple once again defied Crown Authority.

When HM Frigate Rose under Capt. Wallace blockaded Newport, Capt. Whipple, with an armed sloop, chased the Rose's tender ashore on Conanicut island. By this act Whipple "is due the honor of discharging the first gun upon any part of His Majesty's Navy in the American Revolution".

The Rose, was to be heard from again when on October 7, 1775, still under Capt. Wallace, in company with HMS Glasgow and HMS Swan, she bombarded Bristol, Rhode Island. "The night was dark and rainy," says an early historian, "and people were in terror and confusion. For over an hour a hundred and twenty cannon were discharged upon us and kept up a constant fire on the people." Upon cessation of the bombardment, Capt. Wallace demanded and received 100 head of cattle from the town.

Such is the play and drama of history. In 1985 I returned from the Caribbean to Connecticut, and with my Mom and Dad visited the new Rose at Black Rock Park in Bridgeport. Hurricane Gloria had turned northwards and followed me to New England and we took the direct hit of its landfall. We were 3 weeks without power and grateful for the fallen trees as fireplace fuel to warm us for those weeks. Grateful too must be those who sail aboard the Rose, for sure enough the fine pasture oak, which Joshua Slocum so prized for the rebuild of his Spray, also fell in vast numbers before Gloria's winds and much of this was donated to the rebuilding project then underway.

When she anchored up next to me in Bequia, it was as if a small piece of my personal history and my hometown had suddenly resurfaced. Why would "swamp Yankees" go to the trouble to re-build a British ship? Well, why not? History overlaps and grows out of itself and explanations and reasons become as vague as a nations' psyche.

Years after the American Revolution, an ancient Yankee was asked why he had fought at Bunker Hill. TEA? Hell, he never drank the stuff! TAXES? He didn't pay any. TRADE? Blockade didn't bother him much—"but at town meetin' we'd learnt to think for ourselves, to govern ourselves. We wanted to keep it that way."

Likewise at some town meeting the Rose replica as an idea was born and with the help of a few dozen Belizean shipwrights and a tropical hurricane named Gloria, the Rose sails once again and when she arrives in harbor an entire era is re-awakened in our memories. History, as a living story, leaps from the page and takes our breadth away

Maybe that is what "classic" or "vintage" really means. Not some concise formula of age, materials, and rig but a combination of all of these and more, much more. This unknown "quantity" allows the viewer with his mind's eye to conjure an idea of what stories these great tall ships might tell.

BLOODY BAY, JAMAICA, 1983

This bay is haunted: by the Arawaks killed by the Caribs, Caribs killed by the Spanish, Spanish killed by the English…and it is haunted by the pirates killed by the order of their shipmate-turned-King's-man, Henry Morgan. "Negril Harbor" is written on local shore maps, but, with Negril town seven miles to the south, everyone in Jamaica calls it: "Bloody Bay". Whales have also been butchered here…but today the only bloodshed is at dusk and dawn, when a hand connects with a well-fed mosquito attempting lift-off from an arm or ankle.

Haunted bays are great—real quiet. Tranquility here, is broken only by hedonists on horses, from nearby "Club Hedonism"—reported to be the mass-grave-site of an Arawak tribe that left only their hammocks as testimony of ever having lived there. Local people speak of some sacrilege; but life goes on.

In more recent history Henry Morgan packed away his 'Jolly Roger' and the 'privateering' lifefor a pardon and commission from Queen Elizabeth the First to "clean up the buccaneeringalong the coast". So much for "the brotherhood"!

The closest likeness I have seen of some of the most notorious ghosts of Bloody Bay are painted on the walls of a small restaurant-and-bar, almost one-thousand miles to the East, on French Saint Martin. On the walls of "Les Corsaire du Roi" ("Pirates of the King") are three life size paintings of pirates. There is nothing unusual about this, only that two of the portraits are of women! (and if the French weren't tolerant of the exposed breast, these paintings might have been covered-over a long time ago). One of the women pictured is a flaming red-head with matching reddened cutlass! Anne Bonney, 'Calico Jack' Rackham and Mary Read were 'Brigands', yes—but so were Drake, Hawkins and many other a "Devon man", whose applied knowledge and professional skills gave clout to Elizabeth's edicts. These then were all "Pirates of the King"—and had the Spanish defeated the English in 1588, history would have little pity for "English Sea-dogs".

Most of 'Calico Jack's' "freebooters" had done their part to perpetuate the history of slaughter in Bloody Bay, when Henry Morgan directed Captain Jonathan Barnett to "capture and return to Kingston with the pirates". 'Jack' and the 'two ladies' were brought to trial and found guilty by 'The Crown'. He was hung by the neck till not quite dead; drawn by four horses till his arms and legs were dislocated; then exhibited in an iron cage as a barely-living example to other "Brethren of the Coast". 'The ladies', Anne and Mary, were both "with child" and were released.

As far as ghosts are concerned, most of the action is at Bloody Bay. Many a pirate ended a rollicking career on 'Execution Cay' (now Rackham's Cay) in Kingston's 'Port Royal'; but spirits haunt not where they fell, but where they were betrayed.

Things are pretty mellow around here now. Perhaps, like Captain Slocum, one would have to over-eat of cheese (difficult to find here) and plums to witness a visitation…although after some of the local 'overproof' rum, anything is possible.

Notes from the Log:

Surviving the seasons…
Edges of this net like lace in this time of contrasts:
the bombastic and the mundane,
single-mindedness and life's passions,
migrant sailor/noble savage
shipwrecked in the wasteland of contemporary France,
surviving the beasties and heat in tropical America.
Visual encyclopedia:
the Oceanic Society says "garbage put
into the sea outweighs the fish taken out
three to one."
Fusing the transcendental to the commonplace,
a quantum is a set of relation—
ships or an intermediate state,
a piece of "action"
but, symbols do not follow rules of experience.
"Every element of physical reality
must have a counterpart in physical theory,"
said Einstein.
The difference between experience and symbol
is the difference between mythos and logos.
Logos initiates but cannot replace experience.
"Knowledge," wrote e.e. cummings,
"is a polite word for dead but not buried
imagination."
Quantum logic is not based upon the way we think of
things
but upon the way we experience them.

As my friend's grandfather always said,
"after the age of fifty
either show them gold, or tell 'em

a good story."
Tossing poetry and points of view around
like hot potatoes,
I try to remain true to how and why
something was said or written.
I must keep my head out of tin can.
Nevertheless, I have only three options,
rob a bank,
get a job,
or quit complaining!

"One ship drives east, another west
On the selfsame wind that blows,
'tis the set of the sails and not the gales
that defines which way they go'

Like the winds at sea, are the winds of fate
As we wander along in life
'tis the will of the soul
that defines the goal
and not the calm or the strife"

Anon.

THE SUMMER OF '98...CARRIACOU

I am sorry to have to inform you of a distressing development in archaeology here. Three days ago at a construction site in Harvey Vale I recognized what I believe were shards from a burial urn and a cursory inspection of the site revealed many carvings and 'zemi' type artifacts. I approached the foreman who told me I had no right of be on the sight and was driven away.

I contacted the owner of the land and told him that I believed he was soon to uncover much more. He wasn't too interested but that afternoon the first skeleton was found and removed by the workmen and the curious. Later that day many clay bat figures, zemis, bowls, carved stone axes and clay masks and small humanoid stone statues were uncovered and at a depth of almost 6 feet the clay rings of an Indian well almost identical to one discovered some years earlier near the same sight. The owner of the land in the first case was in a hurry to complete their porch so only 7 of the rings were recovered and restored. They are now the centerpieces of the Carriacou museum. The owner of the new sight is a very "progress" oriented type person and work continued.

I attempted to save as much as I could and contacted the historical societies of Carriacou, Grenada, and also called an American woman in St. Vincent who directed the excavation of the first well located at the "Constant spring" guesthouse. Yesterday the 2nd complete skeleton was uncovered and the legs of a 3rd. All at a depth of 6 feet and the entire site is of fine white sand under the dirt and clay.

I am sure there is much to be learned here but the concrete is to be poured today and I really don't have the 3,000 dollars a day to even slow progress a little bit and it upsets me to be so powerless. Local opinion is that it is none of my business and that all 'archaeologists are in it for the big bucks to be gained selling artifacts. The stone human figure described earlier was sold for $15 though I have asked the fellas to please not loot and sell, or if they must (while accusing me of the same and throwing stones at me) to please allow someone from the historical society to photograph them. But nope the right to photos must also be purchased. These were not black or white people but certainly yellow people and probably the original inhabitants, indigenous but dead, buried and most people here wish forgotten. The truth is we know nothing of these people who were most assuredly fine seaman and probably loved their children too.

The cement and 'ree' bar win another round. There was just no time and of course no consolidated effort to stall the construction although I believe an organization like the Worldtrust or the National Geographic people might have been interested but with great haste another guest house and chicken shack will exist in a place which most certainly represented a unique learning experience. I feel that I must apologize to these departed souls for being unable to bring their lives and histories to the attention of those who might have helped but were so far removed in time and curiosity. The cement is being poured daily, probably over 30 yards by now. It seems the historical society here is embarked upon a mission of attempting to recover those items that were recovered by the laborers who spent many hours in the hot sun earning $20 a day hefting shovels and picks. Assuredly many valuable and irreplaceable objects have been removed from the site, but it seems to me to be an example of the analogy of the spilled glass of water, or wine. The glass was tipped and some of the contents have been spilt but the glass is surely still more than half full.

The primary excavation necessitated the removal of hundreds of cubic yards of soil to an average depth of 5 feet and the bulk of this soil is still lying around the edges of the excavation. Would it not seem sensible in light of the excitement and controversy generated by this find to further examine this potential trove of artifacts rather than to further divide the community involved through searches and police surveillance? The piles of dirt surrounding the pits should be thoroughly sifted and this should be monitored by members of the historical society. What is closest to the tops of these piles was recently at the 'bottom' of the hole.

It might even be possible to get some of the students at the local secondary schools and Bishops College involved, thereby insuring some local participation and affording some opportunity for learning from within those institutions dedicated to that goal. One of the skulls was vandalized and smashed perhaps out of a fear born of superstition, certainly not out of hatred, it is almost humanly impossible to hate a dead man. Perhaps this represents an opportunity to celebrate Carriacou as an island that has known human habitation for many thousands of years.

It seems ironic that no attempt has been made to further investigate this site. Before the removal of the circular clay well-head fresh water began to collect in the center ring, yet within hours cement was poured for the construction of a cistern! I may be a bit dense at times but I am unable to understand why this was done, especially on an island notoriously short of water that for 5 months has been in the grips of a drought!

Much speculation exists concerning the presence of human remains. In almost every country in the world if human remains are found, construction is halted so that authorities might determine if any "foulplay' has been committed. In this case with the find at greater than 6 feet and obviously ancient it is probably safe to say no one living today could have had a hand in these peoples deaths. So why are they there? Was there a battle as some people here have conjectured, or was there a plague? I may be wrong but what seems be being overlooked is that this was in all probability a Ceremonial sight, the bodies found here might possibly represent important 'personages' in the lsland-Carib hierarchy. Carib dead were commonly shallowly buried in the houses of relatives and great leaders, healers, navigators were more often placed near a ceremonial site so their 'spirits' might be consulted, either during religious ceremonies or initiation rites. There was even talk of metal weapons being found, but these people had no metal and this site pre-dates any known European presence by close to 1,000 years. As for treasure, or gold, these people had very little, didn't thousands of these people commit suicide rather than be enslaved when they were unable to meet the gold duty imposed by the Spanish and European conquerors. Not until Pizarro and Cortez entered Mexico and Central America did returning ships carry any real treasure.

These were simple people, unsurpassed in seamanship and the 'conuco' type agricultural system that even today has allowed farmers in Cuba to survive in the face of the US embargo, the same farming methods that have been shown to do the least damage to the fragile island eco-systems. Quite possibly these people emigrated from the Amazon Basin long ago, but the wet climate of the rainforest does not give up its' secrets so easily, in fact, archaeology is practically impossible in it's depths. Everything is almost immediately re-absorbed by the jungle, and Carriacou represents the first large relatively dry yet arable regions where "Yuca" or cassava could be successfully cultivated. The name derived from "Yacahu", the name of the supreme creator in these peoples myths, supreme god of Life and Light. This culture traveled extensively as evidenced by the many English and Spanish words derived from their language and similar traditions and myths taught by the-Hichiti, Miccosukee, Muskogee, Taino, Locono, Carib, Arawak and even Mayan peoples.

Most ironic of all…as I walked through this very busy construction site, across the empty bags of cement, I read the brand name on them Arawak! It may not be too late to salvage something here. If teams of historical society members, students, and interested people are able to work together to sort through the pile of debris on the site, perhaps a few of the people responsible for the disappearance of artifacts might come forward to return them to the museum, realizing that this represents a grand opportunity for all the people in the Caribbean to put our differences aside and work towards a greater understanding and hopefully a broader tolerance of the many diversities in this grand "Family of Man."

A LITTLE POLITIC

Several years ago, before what has become known as the Grenada Revolution of 1979, this sailor was pistol-whipped by several "Mongoose Henchmen" who had been given government positions as "Customs Officers". I did not defend myself, but received a rather severe beating. As an American-born, West Indian Cargo-Sloop captain, it was not for me to strike (even in self-defense) an officer wearing the uniform of the Grenada "Customs Service". I was saved from severe injury by a crowd of angry Grenadians who jumped the boatyard fence. "Don't beat de mon; blood is blood," they cried. "You beatin' on de mon 'cause he white. Leave he alone. Blood is blood." Under this protection, I bid a hasty retreat to my vessel and single-handed her to St. Vincent, to put some space between myself and Mr. Gairy's influence.

When I heard of Mr. Bishop's 'bloodless coup' in March of 1979, it was a moment of extreme personal happiness, and I wired my congratulations to the people and Prime Minister. I was in Puerto Rico, having just sailed north from Curacao where I had worked for the season, hauling cargo on my engineless Grenadian Sloop. Since that time, I have been hauling passengers and cargo between the Windwards, Leewards, South-and Central-America, Jamaica, Mexico and the United States. Each year I have been in touch with the Bishop government, letting them know the whereabouts of the Mermaid (she was on the Grenada 35c stamp).

Many of the people of Grenada, (and the associated Grenadines) are seamen. Grenada and the smaller islands of Carriacou and Bequia, have been responsible for the construction of ten times the entire ship-tonnage of all the other Windward-and Leeward-Islands combined (see 'Clean Sweet Wind' by Douglas Pyle, Easy Reach Press). The culture of these islands is based upon an understanding of people who have sailed up and down the "Antillean Chain" in handmade vessels, on seas where the Trade Winds blow at their fullest force. They also share the tribal traditions of small islands, where everyone knows each other, and can trace their lineage to pre-slave Africa. Consequently, the 'local governments' might be best described in analogy to the 'crews of small ships'. The Scottish, Irish and Yankee seamen, whose ships called at these islands in the nineteenth century for crews, left their skills, their lighter skin-tones, and also a tradition of shipboard-ethics.

Democracy is a concept best shared by large, well organized, industrialized societies; who enjoy a degree of stability and prosperity very different from a small, struggling nation. Unfortunately, there was a 'mutiny'. The "Captain-of-State and several Officers were removed from command", and as a "mutinous crew took control of the Ship-of-State", violence and bloodshed again became the rule. It was however, an internal Grenadian dispute, for a people on the rough and rocky road to political stability and independence. I was shocked to hear of the deaths of Mr. Bishop, his Ministers and the innocent people involved. Perhaps I was more shocked to hear about U.S. Ranger-paratroopers suddenly turned loose on Grenada. When the Southern Caribbean suffered hurricane damage during the seasons from 1979 to 1981, the U.S. established a 'commission' to investigate the situation.

Cuba sent doctors, engineers, tractors, food, tools and, yes, some 'advisors'; but people in a sinking ship take their help where they can find it. When basic-aid was needed, the U.S. and her allies were not to be heard from. Too bad that, when the U.S. finally came to the "assistance", of this small and beautiful nation, they came with the 'cavalry'.

Mr. Bishop realized the principal problems of leading his "tribe" but he also gave the people a dream of real freedom that few other nations could have understood.

WINDWARD, CARRIACOU, 1984

It is post Carriacou Regatta and Mermaid sits comfortably to a long chain, made fast to second-mate "Dr. Jekyl" (the two hundred and fifty pound 'insurance policy' this vessel carries at her starboard cathead).

Windward (or Watering Bay) is a superb all-weather shelter, with tiers of barrier reefs in all directions. If the "monster" anchor should drag, I'm in a good spot to get some 'bottom work' done; there are more shipwrights than bartenders in this community. It was a wonderful week for the "workboat" fancier. The vessels are from eleven to fifty feet. Most are without motor, and carry enough sail to stir "J-Boat" fantasies in the traditionalist: Water-sails, Drifters, Spinnakers, Sprits'ls and Gaffs. However the oddest thing this sailor encountered was the largest collection of warships the Mermaid has anchored with since a visit to Key West. In fact, the U.S.S. Simms Fast Frigate No. 1059 (which gave a gala flare-salute to all vessels on the first day of the regatta) arrived from sea in Key West (on December 1, 1983) the same day as the Mermaid. It is a small ocean!

Many paths are crisscrossed because of this rootless style, but not since my days in the U.S. Navy Hospital Corps have I been so aware of the sound of helicopters in the morning rain. Most of the people here are grateful to the U.S., for guaranteeing their freedoms as seamen and community businessmen. The main dock in Hillsborough is well on the way to completion. It should greatly facilitate the loading and discharge of both cargo and passengers. As one of the satellite states of Grenada, Carriacou had long been neglected by the Central Government. The roads here have not been maintained since Mr. Herbert

Blaize\a resident of Carriacou) was Grenada's Prime Minister; in the era before the dark days of Mr. Eric Gairy's "Mongoose Gang" rule.

The sea, that 'road' with which all Grenadine residents are intimately familiar, has been kind. Not since Hurricane "JANET" in 1955 have these islands been seriously threatened. Today, at Windward and Harvey Vale, four separate vessels (35–80 feet) are being prepared, for the day when—"to the chanteyman's cry"—they will be bodily pulled into the sea, to join their cousins in the largest "working" fleet I have seen in my years of cruising.

As in Bedouin society, there is no mechanism here by which unearned privilege can be maintained. The sea does not play favorites. Four people drifted forty miles west of Carriacou in a thirteen foot Boston Whaler, and were subsequently rescued on the second day of the Regatta by the tug' Christine F.', in a combined United States Coast Guard and civil search. They have seen a side of "small boat economics" that few people live to tell about "the cheering of the arena is seldom heard during the concentration of mind and spirit on the event". It is a day-by-day struggle to—exercise and thereby protect—an individual's freedom; whether it be 'freedom of the sea' or 'the right to vote'. "Truth" for the people of these islands is work. "Truth" is apprenticeship, pain, effort, sweatand blood. "Truth" isn't an argument, or a correct phrase that's "lawyers' truth". Who knows a greater liar than a lawyer? There's "city truth" and there's "country truth"; there's lawyers truth" and "human truth"; "thought-up truth" and "lived truth".

MERMAIDS DON'T USE
DECIMALS

The decimal system is basically a French innovation. Part of General Chauvin's plan for a unified Europe and written as the Napoleonic Code—better known as 'Chauvinism'. The meter is one ten-millionth of the circumference of the earth with the great circle (meridian) passing through both poles and Paris. Real neat, but does it work? Nope. For example a nautical mile is still one sixtieth of three-hundred-and-sixty parts of the Equatorial circle or 6,080 feet. No decimals, and there will always be 360 degrees in a circle—right?

As for money—"coin-of-the-realm", most people will say most currencies are decimal already. Are there not 100 cents or centimes or centavos in the dollar, franc or peso? But there exists, in East Caribbean, Canadian and American currencies that most unlikely of coins: the 'quarter'. And this quarter is not .25 of 100 but 2/8 of 8/8. This "2-bit" coin in its conception and history bears testimony to the once internationally accepted "silver piece-of-eight", the pre-eminent coin of the Christian world for over 200 years. Just as the ancient Romans once paid in "salt", hence salary for work usually in a measure of "avoir-du-pois" or "what's in the can" or the net contents or real worth etc. I've always felt better throwing in my "two-bits" worth than my "two-cents" worth. Speaking "sailor-to-sailor" now, everyone knows that 8/8 is equivalent to 100% and makes a whole, but conversely 8 eights are 64 and is it not true that a ship as property consist of 64 shares and not one or ten or one hundred?

I guess what I'm trying to say is that weights and measures be damned, two bits will always to me be worth more than two and a half

40

dimes and where I live a litre of the most common form of water weighs more than a kilo; when weather approaches it does so in knots not kilometers per hour; a pound of gold is heavier than 454 grams of feathers and one ounce of good sense is worth more than 28.3 grams of almost anything else including even one Troy ounce of gold weighing 30.16 grams or 0.82286 pounds (avoirdupois of course)—that's one twelfth written 1/12, one of twelve, and I'm not talking about eggs or dozens! As for rum, I'll always prefer to buy an eighth or "gill" which in the British imperial system is equal to five fluid ounces, ¼ pint or 28.423 millilitres, but just because monkeys have ten fingers doesn't mean they hold their liquor any better, an old fisherman in St. Croix once told me: "Monkey shouldn't play wid musket", but an even wiser old "Kayak" insists to me that the oldest right for a man in the West Indies, is "the right to walk home drunk"!

BAG—O—TRICKS

Generations of my 'water-men' kin have inhabited the waterfront, together with the muskrats, raccoons, fishes and other foolish, still-hardy types that have not yet succumbed to the ease, air-conditioning and fluorescent-light pallor of the city dweller. My uncle had often been in trouble for keeping his shotgun filled with rock salt. He used it to keep 'dumpers' from fouling up the waters of the Housatonic River in Connecticut, where he kept his vessel the Bag of Tricks.

Recently, I heard that the Rainbow Warrior of "Greenpeace" was sabotaged and sunk in New Zealand; with the loss of a man's life, and the photographic records of countless confrontations in the fight to maintain a 'Nuclear-free Zone' in the Pacific.

Somehow these two events have meshed: perhaps a little painfully. If by "nuclear" we mean "centered and together in thought, dream and action", I'm for it: but if Strontium-90 in the breast milk of every human female and in the bones of all vertabrae on earth, radioactive gasses, and half-lives of 2.15 million years are involved; well it kind of touches my life, my home, the Caribbean…and my life style as a 'sea-roamer' in particular. Jacques Cousteau labeled the Caribbean "The most endangered sea in the world".

There are always those who will be cynical about any 'grassroots effort' to prevent the molestation of any ocean, forest or even social structure. West Indians are often cynical but, as V.S. Naipual said in 'The Middle Passage'…if a society breeds cynicism it also breeds toler-ance…tolerance for every human activity and affection for every dem-onstration of wit and style". Individual "wit and style" is what marked my Uncle Bob's attempts to protect "his river"…And it is "wit and style", (coupled with a worldwide grassroots environmental concern) which most distinguishes those that were involved with Rainbow Warrior in the vanguard of ecological concern.

While cruising from "upsouth" (that is to say, while Northbound with sheets-slacked) my attention was caught by what appeared to be a vessel either dumping, or hauling, large objects over the side. Being the curious sort, I altered course and investigated. Instead of the "pirate dumper" I had first suspected, I came up to a medium-large Freighter "fishing", or harpooning porpoises. Well, "a man's gotta eat"…but I was a little heartsick. I know people have hunted whales in the Caribbean for years; but coming upon this act at-sea was a bit of a shocker! I went on my way a sadder, but wiser, man.

I anchored up in Charlestown, Nevis, and saw the "fishing freighter" at the dock. The crewman I spoke to was at first hesitant to talk of "the fishing", until I pointed out the Mermaid as my vessel, when suddenly I was on the "in" with the whole crew. These were all nice guys, doing what comes naturally. The Caribbean man is often a seaman, and therein lies the male sporting-activity 'par excellence'. Fishing is a "totally-significant activity", which supplies both protein and prestige. There wasn't much I could say really, except to draw on a few superstitions about seamens' luck and the historical (though Hellenic) view that Dolphins and Whales are somewhat special in the pantheon of life. Without calling on some 'duppie', or risking alienating fellow seamen I really couldn't do much. But I did try to make a point and a little bit of superstition may just be another one of the tools from my bag-of-tricks. It may not have been very "witty and stylish", but I was there and did what I could.

I would be sad, however, if public concern for the ocean-environment caused those people closest to it—the fishermen, the sailors, the 'water' people—to be legislated into nonexistence. 'Busting' a sailboat or an individual fishing boat does not solve any problems; it buries them in red tape. As individuals, we've got to be concerned and dedicated to "the truth"—that there are some things money can't buy, and some lessons that law enforcement can't teach. If the Caribbean as a sea, and the West Indies as a social system, are to be saved; the task will be accomplished on a person-to-person basis.

Archives: Associated Press
MATARI BAY, New Zealand

The Greenpeace ship Rainbow Warrior was deliberately scuttled Saturday by the environmental group years after French spies sank the vessel in Auckland's harbor. The patched and rusting ship was towed to the Cavalli islands off New Zealand's northern tip and sunk in 60 feet of water to become an artificial reef and symbolic diving memorial. "It's a fitting end for a ship that tried so long to protect the environment", a Greenpeace spokesman said. The converted 400-ton fishing trawler was surrounded by a flotilla of spectator craft as it slipped below the waves. Hours earlier, a Greenpeace member tried to chain himself to the Rainbow Warrior to prevent the scuttling, the New Zealand Press Association said.

In 1985, the French government ordered the ship sunk to prevent it from leading a protest flotilla to a French nuclear testing site in the South Pacific. French divers used mines to tear apart the ship's hull as it sat in Auckland's harbor. A Greenpeace photographer was killed. The episode triggered a major diplomatic row between France and non-nuclear New Zealand. Two French agents involved were captured and convicted of sabotage. Maj. Alain Mafart and Capt. Dominique Prieur were ordered jailed for 10 years but later released to French custody in exchange for $ 10 million, an apology, and the lifting of a trade ban on New Zealand imports.

AQUATIC SCHMOO?

I just don't think it is fair to portray whales as some type of aquatic "schmoo" (pardon my reference to Andy Capp's "Li'l Abner"): friendly, intelligent, happy; non-threatening, available, easily-killed and delicious. Why not try to protect a small part of the "whole" and why not protect creatures that are affable, intelligent, happy and kindly to human beings?

The primary reason for the IWC allowance of two or three whales to countries like St. Vincent is to protect the traditional and mostly self-conserving technique of open, sail powered boats and hand-thrown harpoons, pursuing (often far offshore) the occasional Humpback or Sperm whale but this is not the case in regards to the hunting and sale of the porpoises and pilot whales (blackfish). These are much smaller, often easier to approach, especially with a high speed boat using deck mounted cartridge-firing harpoon guns. I personally have seen fisher vessels with a 20-foot blackfish hung from each gunwale and an open hold of smaller porpoises. Such things are not so uncommon or else the cetacean products industry in Trinidad (soap and margarine made with "marine fat") would not be so successful. The fact is, there would not have been a local market for the approximately 8,000 pounds of black-fish Landed at Bernoulli, St. Vincent, on 23 August this year. Certainly a small amount of blackfish is consumed locally, but most is probably exported. That's my main "beef", not that I don't understand the tra-dition, skill, danger and honor inherent in open-boat whaling as prac-ticed in Bequia. It's that I am shocked at whaling for an export market. Lots of my friends own a piece of scrimshaw—usually a Pilot's tooth on a string—and the etchings are often superb. Heck, maybe the whale lost the tooth naturally and is still okay (they have 66 you know). But when I think of little cans—and I know they're out there—with whales meat and blubber inside, I get a bit worried.

WEEKS OF CALM AND COAXING THE BOAT

Spinning in circles as wind shifts. I was hoping to get to St. Barths but now the wind 'backs' into the North so the Mermaid settles into Great Bay, St. Maarten with word of Tropical Storm "Barry". Crew is working on Ground-tackle and sails. I have not been 'off-the-boat' for two weeks, but feeling fine surrounded by the boat and what I have and what I really need; rather than being 'on-the-beach' surrounded by the eminently desirable (but usually over-rated and over-priced) pleasures, without which I seem to get along well enough. So, good sense prevails, as the moon fills and the nights lengthen.

TROPICAL STORM "CHANTEL"

Offshore fishing—onboard living, swimming miles.

TROPICAL STORM "DEAN"

Looks like it might pass close with 60 knot winds, so on 1st August, into the Lagoon in St. Maarten. 'Boat Jail'! A squall line "hits like bricks" while I am at the 'Mahogany Reef' of the 'Turtle Pier Bar'. So, I shoot back through choppy seas and rain [stomach trembles at this awesome truth approaching]. But the storm turns North (after sinking the dinghy with rain) and so I swim to neighboring Yacht Bayadheere and, with friends unwind with wine and salad.

Row the mile to Marigot (for bird-seed and to watch the street life) as I remain stranded in 'the pond', listening to reports of Tropical Storm "Gabrielle"…which also passes North. I must get out of here! So underway solo, to the Virgin Islands and Jost Van Dyke and Wooden Boats and old friends…and reports of tropical storm "Hugo"…which does not pass North.

I move Mermaid into the shelter of the Mangroves in Hurricane Hole, St. John. So here I am, very free and very well-anchored in the midst of the Mangroves, surrounded by friends: Anuanua—Wanderlust—Winifred—Poetry—Windborne and Aquarius but feeling very alone as "hugo" increased its proportion of day to day trauma/reality, for it is no longer a 'drill'. Saturday 16th September "Hugo" well Southeast gusting 130 mph and coming. Wind here from West-Northwest at 12 to 15 knots...till Sunday 17th September, and the 'bottom falls out'.

Gusting 50...

now 70...

now 120...

now its' just indescribable!!! as Winifred breaks loose,

Aquarius busts her Cleats and smashes into Anuanua; So through the night till dawn the winds are at 100+ from Northwest!!

But we are through the worst of it.

Reports of over 300 boats damaged in Culebra and over 150 sunk! Here, the Xebec and Misty Law were destroyed, and every boat in Coral Bay was on the road. Vet. G.I.'s patrol the town and east-end of St. John, because of looting. There are no roads, no power—and not a leaf on any tree.

I tried to calm the woman who found the body of a dead man on the yacht Texas Tea. I did not know the man, but we are all in need of some comfort...and lose track of time. But with the help of friends (with so much work to be done) life looks less fragile, and in the cool morning clearness we re-open our eyes and become light's witness.

LETTER

Things mighty quiet around here, as the sign at the "Tiki WIL-LIN Bar" says—"a whole lot of Nuttin' going on", the volcano ain't the only thing sleeping but, after several months in the Virgin Islands that pace is just about right. I was looking forward to attending the "Sweethearts" Race in Tortola but a nice light SW Breeze a few days before put me in the mind to head NE—away from the piles of "Hurricane Hugo" residue I had been livin with at the Independent Boat Yard; Wednesday nites with "mighty-whitey", and cold American Beer but it was nice to leave on a reach to the East. I did some zig-zagging thru Pillsburg Sound in company with Peter Holmberg—Filming a TV Commercial for the Virgin Islands Tourist Bureau. Seems there ain't many West Indian Vessels around and "Mermaid of Carriacou" just fit the ticket for the film makers—especially with my new red Mainsail, blue & white Jib—white topsides and blue Bottom-the olde "Red, White & Blue". I figure I'll try to sell the same idea to the French Tourist Bureau on St. Barths, but call it Blue, White and Red. If that works I'll try it again with the Dutch—this time calling the Boat White, Red and Blue.

The wind fell light a bit SW of Anegada so I got on the VHF and called Lowell Wheatley at "Anegada Reef Hotel" to verify the 5 sec. white flasher as W end of Anegada—sure enough that's the light, but Lowell said to be cool cause the light is about 1/2 mile up the Beach! So we got Mermaid about 20 miles N of the same flash and the wind just stopped. Flat calm...so we dropped all gear and wrapped aluminum foil around a few ballast "rock—stones" and played time the decent for a few hours till a wall of weather to the NW promised plenty of wind. We got it; whew, probably 50 knots on "Valentines Day"—must'a been a scene for the Sweethearts!

Well we fetched up St. Maarten in about 15 hours we pumped a bit, (we wore out a few Whale 25 pump parts) but had no gear failures and I figure if I had of re-lead the pump discharges out of the stern we might of cut another hour off of the trip—kinda like an "afterburner". But anyway, a bad day sea is better than a good day at the boatyard, and a perfect day fishin south of Nevis takes the edge off of any passage—especially now that the hot spring baths in Bath Village, Nevis are open once again…Fifteen minutes in these volcanic pools will turn the most salty sailor into a bowl of jelly—mighty fine! Haven't caught but one 'Dorado' for the week but dozens of "Sabre Toothed Grunts" (Barracuda), I just throw dem back when in the Leewards. Being no Beauty anyway I'd sure not look any better bald, as wise olde "Marius" at Le Select says "I wouldn't eat them if you caught 'em in front of the church!" A couple of local guys here ask me to bring these saber toothed beasts in for their pot, but my conscience would sure plague me if anyone got sick and suffered the agony of ciguatera poisoning.

Perhaps if I get back to the Virgin Islands, I'll go shark fishing what with all the reports of increased sightings there. No surprise really; I mean the Virgin Islands is one of the few places in the world that protects the turtles and if I can see half a dozen on a short swim this information has got to have reached the sharks which gobble them up. It is hard to protect the environment without supporting a few of the unsavory predators! And on a similar note, I hear the charter season there is a bit slack, well with all the hoopla about all "de mash-up vessels", and all the insurance claims and "FEMA" money spent, the natural conclusion of any statesider is that the place was trashed. Odd isn't it, that the B.V.I., which did not have so much of an insurance scam going on and thereby received less disaster aid has been booked solid!—The olde lesson of not being able to have your cake and eat it too.

This fishing ain't easy! Even not catching anything is as much work as catching a lot, and no matter how hard I try I always poke my fingers a Bit—twisting leaders, rigging Baits, etc.—Makes for some sore fingers—which is why those olde toothpaste tubes are so handy—just clean em out, pack'em over the sore appendage and you've got a "waterproof—flexible—digit wrapper"; but with all the poop about fluorides who knows what other complications might develop! We was all of us fishermen, sipping some rum at the end of the other day and there wasn't one of us without at least one finger cut—and no-one here takes days off. The fish take days off but the 'zen' of living long enough to become an "olde man of the sea" enforces a regimen of early mornings and long afternoons, full bellies and deep sleep. The "Great Dimaggio" may be gone…but somewhere the lions still play on the beach in Africa and the "Big One" is still out there. 90% of this fishing game is having a bait in the water.

TRAUMATIC STRESS SYNDROME—REVISITED

Believing that Hurricane "Hugo" would be the penultimate event which could possibly involve the Mermaid...not disregarding the fact that the boatyard travel lift blew a tire an dropped the boat after several weeks on the 'Hard'—necessitating a 'next' haulout...I sailed into the '90's hoping for (and firmly believing in) a short respite from the 'shit-happens' syndrome. Hah! I should have known better I have held onto that well known sailors' credo which states "Hope for the best, but be ready for the worst". So—imbued with the energy of the ecstasy of the escape from months in the boatyard—Mermaid and Crew set forth once again, hard on the wind, rail down but with "peckers-up" attitude to join with whatever unexpected events bound to happen.

Three days South from Anguilla...totally becalmed for over 32 hours in the lee of Guadeloupe. The crews of 2, nursing images of the Grenadines, were getting a bit "squirrelly". After all, the Capt. (me) had estimated a total run of maybe 60 hours to Bequia, and here we were watching French TV from the Basseterre Lee, with neither crois-sants nor fish. Lots of "rock and roll", but of the maritime kind. A 'pre-venter' worked loose on the 34 foot long Boom during a particularly vicious roll (we had to tie down the TV), and (with deep-forest sound) the Boom shattered in the center, very luckily injuring no-one. No wind and now no boom! Still no croissants, and going into the third day of watching the morning traffic from 3 miles out. Becalmed, drift-ing and fishing very deep indeed!

The wind picked up that afternoon and with a loose-footed reefed Mainsail we turned North and considered our options. We were able to lay Antigua, which we reached the next morning. Now Mermaid has never really behaved like a 'Swan'; she's more of a "wood-duck"; and now with a "broken wing", she was having a time-of-it getting into the East and the shelter of Falmouth Harbour. We 'spoke' a Dutch-Flag Container ship, which was willing to take us into St. John's harbor. The crew was anxious to get ashore anywhere, but had not suffered the trauma of ever trying to 'pass a line' to a 500 foot-long ship: so, much to the crews' chagrin, we kept her strapped down and short-tacked towards less readily attained but more secure of a sanctuary. By this time, many people had picked up bits of our radio conversations and were wondering what price the two 'crew' would pay to walk on anything but Mermaid's deck.

We weren't sinking; had no physical injuries; there was plenty of food and water; plus, once again, proximity to land had taken the 'bite' out of the sea. I've lived aboard now for 21 years, 15 on the Mermaid, and there wasn't really anywhere to go, so I was quite willing to spend another few days getting into port'under my own power'. The crew however were on "thin ice", so we ultimately accepted a tow from the Jenny B, (a local fisherboat) and by nightfall that day were comfortably anchored-up in front of the Antigua Yacht Club. After all, we were Yachting, after a fashion.

It's amazing how fast a crew can disperse! Single-handed once again, I commenced to make repairs and in 2 weeks was ready to continue South. A couple on their 25th wedding anniversary, wishing to visit Dominica, signed aboard. Soon thereafter salt spray once again graced my decks—'Port-tack' at 6 knots thru the night…And 35 miles West of Basseterre we were once again becalmed!

Hundreds of porpoises swam around us, and we all three were soon overboard, in the water, trying to interpret their whistles and clicks. The porpoises, for their part, seemed to enjoy the idea of these humans taking time from their very human-race to play with them…Such are the blessings of non-scheduled cruising and open-eyed waiting.

I had been painting quite a picture of Dominica for my guests, and they were quite excited about arriving there; but we had drifted some 15 miles farther West and the wind, which was just beginning to pick up, was from the Southeast. I had read once (in a 'Hornblower' novel) that if you want to go eastward in the Caribbean you had best keep on the 'Starboard-tack'…but this would only succeed in getting us back into the lee of Guadeloupe. So rather than repeat that performance, I began to cultivate an interest (on their behalf) in the island of St. Lucia; which, as well as being much greener than Antigua (but less spectacular than Dominica) was straight ahead!

They loved St. Lucia and the combination of the anchorage behind what was once Pidgeon Island with the ease of 'Clearance' and proximity to a pizza restaurant, made me forget whatever "difficulties" I once might have had with the harbor and the authorities in Castries.

I'm almost there now and (though I was unable to find crew in Rodney Bay) I felt that the last hundred miles or so to Carriacou would be a balm to "soothe olde wounds", and put the horror of "HUGO", boatyards, broken spars and neurotic crews behind me. The spiritually refreshed and freshly provisioned, I set forth (alone) hoping to arrive in time for the Carriacou Regatta in early August. At 1700 on the 2nd of August I was 3 miles west of The Pitons…and totally becalmed…and so I was to remain all that night. I dropped all sails, rigged a deck light, and went below to get an 'Offshore weather' broadcast; and to watch some of the 'Goodwill Games' on CNN—live from Seattle! Itlooked windy in Seattle—There was not a breath near St. Lucia. At 06.30 on the 3rd, Tropical Storm "CEASAR" was located well to the East and North, while a tropical wave was located to the East with it's axis at 55 degrees West; wind will soon come! In the meantime however, calm, it was like something out of Coleridge, except the only "scaly beast" was my parrot "Bonacca" who really didn't give adamn. He has been aboard all his life (and there is no place like home) and if you are a jungle bird the lack of a fair sailing breeze does not affect you at all.

It's times like these that try a sailor's strength! Is it better to drop everything and just drift (while waiting for the wind) or should the singlehander behave like a complete fool and try to set a spinnaker? I opted for 'working sails', a double reefed main, light genoa foresail, and a yankee cut jib tops'l, everything in topping-lifts and rigged with preventers…stillabout 700 sq. feet of sail. But, with preventers on the gaff and boom, it is not too unwieldy if there is not a lot of sea—which there wasn't.

At 09.00 that morning, just ghosting along at 2 knots and steering 200 degrees compass, well clear of any danger (except for northern St. Vincent well into the East and 15 miles distant) I went below to fix some breakfast and to make a pot of tea. After which, there still being no wind, I sat in a corner (too comfortable a corner it seems, for I did indeed doze off) and did not waken 'till nearly three hours later, when (the approaching wave having shifted the wind to the North) Mermaid driving along at 6 knots, had come to a sudden crashing halt as she attempted to push Fancy Point, St. Vincent, to the East of it's charted position!!! Had I grounded 50 yards to Starboard I would now have been on a small beach, and 50 yards to Port I would have been on a breaking reef. Suddenly out of the undergrowth arrive 3 fishermen who, while shouting at me for being a fool or drunk (or both), mounted the cliff (at the base of which Mermaid had struck) and commenced to forcibly "by hand" push the vessel away from the shore. So now I'm 50 feet from the cliff (with no stem, foredeck or bowsprit) and, with every lifting-sea, gallons of seawater are flooding into the foc'sle. I cut the lashings on the 250 lb fisherman anchor and let it go. I would not be able to let out much scope; the cliff, beach, and rocks were very close and (as so often happens behind high islands) the wind was now blowing onshore (from the West). Fortunately my battery-bank was fully charged, so I switched on both electric pumps and put two of the fishermen on the Whale 25 pumps. I grabbed my "T-50" staple-gun (loaded with 1/2 inch staples), I cut away most of the now destroyed jib sail and, with a safety line around my waist, jumped overboard in an attempt to fother the large hole which had been the upper stem.

About 10 minutes (and hundreds of staples) later the largest part of the hole is roughly covered and I climb back aboard to discover that both of the manual pumps have been broken by their over-zealous operators. Now to get the "raffel" cleared away, and to convince the 2 small fishing boats which have arrived on the scene that (with their combined force of their 6 and 14 horsepower motors) we are able to pull the vessel out to sea, away from the rocks and reef. The fishermen think that I should beach the boat and attempt repairs, but I know in my heart that I would rather see her sink than see her painfully and slowly destroyed in the surf; her bones picked clean by the "vultures" on the beach.

So to sea—1/2 mile. My new 'crew' (the 3 fishermen who helped so much by jumping aboard) are now scared for their lives, believing the vessel must sink…The Capt. has gone back over-the-side with his staple-gun…after issuing to the entire crew lifejackets, and cutting-away the lashings on the two lifeboats. Whilst over-the-side, I hear an approaching motorboat: then discover that my 'crew' is abandoning ship, grabbing whatever is not tied-down and throwing it all in the motorboat.

Once again, the fishermen attempt to convince me to put the boat on the beach; but I am deaf to such an idea and resume my work below with the stapler, and listen to the departing boat. Several yachts pass during the next 8 hours, but all either ignore or misinterpret my signals, flares, smoke and "Maydays'.

Finally, the French cruising yacht Jane of Marseilles lowers its sails and comes to my assistance. And, after I am satisfied with my temporary patch-job they pass a line and take me in-tow to Wallabaloo Bay, 10 miles farther down the coast.

The Customs officer in Wallabaloo is sorry to hear about my accident, but must do her duty. So, I am duly 'Cleared-in', and issued a 'Cruising permit'. The crew of the Jane and I return to the Mermaid (now tied comfortably, stern to the coconut trees) and, with wooden battens and more of the blown-out jib, strengthen the patch on the 'Stem'.

After dinner aboard the 'Jane', I return to the pumps, and sleep a few hours before we get underway in the morning. They have only a 15 hp diesel, but it is still very calm and now I am able to use my mainsail (I only pray that it stays calm for the crossing over to Bequia). Halfway across the channel the current and wind pick up but, fortunately, the motor vessel Little Grand has come alongside and taken over the tow from the Jane.

By mid-day on Friday Mermaid is anchored in Admiralty Bay and, with the help of "speedy-John" of Gaucho, we double up the patches with more cloth and battens…and make ready for the next leg of Mermaid's return to Carriacou.

Under conditions such as these, when "all hangs in the balance" (but there is a balance; if only a tenuous one) it's nice to be in a "sailors' port" and know there is time to grab a Green Boley Roti and a cold beer. "Pour some out for the spirits", here at the gates of the Grenadines—the islands of seamen, who know what it means when they tell you: "It is better to be born lucky than to be born rich"…

It was here in Bequia, that morning at 'The Green Boley', that Nolly Simmons repeated a story I had heard the night before (but in French) while aboard the Jane; about Bernard Moitessier and his vessel the Marie-Therese, that hit that same cliff and so was spared the agony of either the beach or reefs. As if the spirits of long-dead, long-suffering Carib seamen, who had leapt from the same or similar cliff, facing the end of their culture, had pity upon we (brave/foolish sailors-of-today) who think on them as we enter their kingdom…"this land of reefs". Bernard remained at his masthead till his vessel sank, and only then did he swim to the beach.

It's still 35 miles to Carriacou. I've jury-rigged a strop at the lower 'bobstay-tang', which marks the low end of what once was the stem, but is now a "window with the curtains drawn". With this strop I am able to fly an "almost-stem-staysail" and I'm underway on a long line thru a block in Gaucho's mizzen-boom end (traditional Colin Archer rescue). At 08.00 on Sunday 5th August we're under way…and the weather holds! By 16.00 we're into Hillsborough Harbor, and I let loose the towline so Mermaid can sail herself into the anchorage.

The next day I enter the swimming competition (as if it were penance for the long swim I didn't have to make to St. Vincent that Moitessier did make). I barely finished…and dead last! I am exhausted, and all of me hurts; but life, limbs and boat are all more or less holding themselves together.

With Speedy's help we get the Mermaid over to Windward and, like a long-wandering sea turtle that has found the beach of it's birth, I realize how lucky I was…and how much work there is to do. I spent almost two months collecting timber before I did much more than "stabilize the patient". Iron-mangrove root for 'Hanging-and-Lodging-Knees'. White-Cedar for the three 'Deck-Beams' that were shattered. More cedar for 'Knightheads' and more Mangrove for the 'Breast-hooks'. It is no longer possible to buy good Central-American Yellow-Pine—called Bonacca-Pine in Honduras—but I had a few planks left from my cruise out in that direction, and Zeph McClaren (the vessel's builder) had some 'spare parts' in his basement.

There never were many power tools involved in boat-building here (Windward not get electricity until just 6 years ago). But as Doug Pyle said in his book, Clean Sweet Wind "if it's boatbuilding you want, it's Carriacou you going". Progress is just that; a 'progression', and rarely have I been in a place where each and every day the tangibles of daily bread and thanksgiving go so hand-in-hand.

I wanted to let everyone know that Mermaid is still in "the longer race"; and to say thanks to the many people who did what they could to help out. My only regret is that the few possessions that were stolen probably did not get to those who helped the most and to those who will continue to sail along in spite of horror stories like this one…"Hope for the best—but be ready for the worst"…I'm buying another staple-gun, and will always "spill a drop" for those who weren't so lucky…Hard luck is better than no luck at all.

MAIL FOR THE GODDESS

Months since a note. Up to my neck in a relationship of the most heated and poisonous of proportions. Sheltering and sharing the simple pleasures of hearth and home, but complicated by three distinct and separate dictionaries. Never before did I believe that an assumed mutual understanding could leave me so misunderstood. Without shoes, I leave no trail this high above the tide line, but wonder: should I kick a tree with my steel-toed boots and leave a mark the sea will not disturb? The rain has obliterated the craters of my tears, and the salty sandy darkened orbits of my eyes question the burning light and the mud in my mouth. It is not in me to becry inequality in this scrying place I have often sought, yet never acknowledged

If belief is futile and desire our burden, I shall find it hard to fly again. For I have traveled in freedom upon the Ocean too long, and this new science which wishes to possess me with a pilgrims ardency might well ring hollow on the morn. For it seems the Goddess likes, even demands, that her novitiates swim in the sink of melancholy. Creation is fire—Culture its coal. Yet people will believe anything about a man (especially anything that shows he hasn't behaved himself about money, women or rum) and on television the good guy always wins, so most people believe all winners are good guys—This is not always the case. But once a habit is developed, effort is replaced by spontaneity. So instead of having the attention hold the object, the object holds the attention.

ALL EXCEPT THE SOAP ON
A ROPE

For the most part the expression or command 'hand me that rope', when heard aboard a boat will generate confusion and not a small amount of disdain. 'Hand' is certainly a verb, but aboard a ship it means to 'furl' or 'reef a sail', and most sailors will tell you that there are no ropes on a ship except perhaps the one around the neck of a mutineer when hung from a yard!

Sailors use very definitive terms for particular pieces of rope or line, depending upon their particular function as a sheet, halyard, anchor rode, preventer etc, but you all knew that! Did you know though, that there are in fact nine ropes aboard a sailing vessel...and they are:

Bell Rope a short hand-rope secured to the clapper of the ships' bell.

Foot Rope a rope stretched under the yards and jib-booms, for men to stand on while loosing or furling the sails. Also the rope sewn to the lower edge of a sail.

Bolt Rope a rope sewn all the way around the edge of a sail to prevent the canvas tearing.

Man Rope safety ropes, rigged alongside ladders, steep steps or any hazardous area.

Top Rope a rope used to hoist and lower a topmast.

Back Rope a rope or chain for staying the 'Dolphin Striker' or 'Martingale'.

Yard Rope a rope used for hoisting or lowering yards which are usually left in position. The equivalent rope for a lowering yard is a halyard.

Bucket Rope you know that one!

Tiller Rope a rope connecting the tiller head to the barrel of the steering wheel. Usually untarred 25 thread yarn of three or four strands, with or without a heart, and which is laid harder than other ropes.

So there you have it, I hope that everyone 'Knows the Ropes' a bit better now but more important, are the verbs used to define the working of a line, rope, sheet or halyard.

Several years ago, in Admiralty Bay harbor in Bequia, I was asked to help the captain of the fine wooden gaff-cutter, 'Just-Now' mount his mast head in a bosun chair so that he could inspect his running rigging. We both recognized the importance of a chair with a crossed bridle beneath, safety lines, and of course staying 'out from under' should a marlin spike or a crescent wrench fall. We even went so far as to cover his solar panels with plywood, and to cover or close all hatches, but we had not worked out our verbs.

I sat on the foredeck, reclining in the jib waiting for instructions from above, when the cry 'un-slacken the rope' reached my ears. I shouted up the mast for clarification, and once again heard the same cry 'un-slacken' the rope. Well I 'un-slackened' the rope, by hauling on it which almost, very nearly almost 'pitch poled' Capt. Bowman over the mast head. Well that's what he had said, and repeated!

Intuitively I had known that he had wanted to come down but, his insistence on repeating an absolutely improper verb elicited from me a slightly mischievous response. His command to 'let me down, let me down' prompted me to 're-slacken' the halyard and lower him to the deck. He was vexed, but unharmed. He had a safe chair and a life line remember! It took better than one half bottle of rum between us until he too saw the humor in my response. Fortunately, there were no other crew or officers around to go 'fetch a rope' and I was not hanged from his spreaders for my mutinous behavior.

JUST STAY CALM

Being becalmed has its advantages and dis-advantages. When underway we appear to reach our goals as islands rise to our vision from under the horizon and a voyage fills with the cycle of departure—time enroute and landfall, but only when becalmed can we linger in the soft smells of charcoal smoke and rain or mist fresh from the upper peaks occasionally scented with a whiff of sulphur from one of the many active volcanoes. The smell of towns reach our decks often touched by the scent of fresh baked bread and not infrequently we are joined by a pod of small whales who kindly suffer the intrusion of we who share a similar joyous nature and boundless curiosity.

Maybe one finds what one seeks, but more often than not, being confused or even downright 'lost' offers even more intriguing opportunities and learning experiences. Maybe we suddenly understand an eternal truth, maybe we resolve a personal struggle—cutting one more fiber of the web that binds us to what we believe, freeing us a small bit more, making us more able to learn something new, see things a little differently. Maybe we make a friend but just as often we discover that who we think are our friends are not. Allies yes, for every obstacle offers opportunity to improve ourselves. A swift kick is often as important helping hand to keep us on the path, on our way and the virtue of patience is often confused with the vice of sloth.

I've been on my way or rather along 'this' way as an off-becalmed cruising sailor for over 30 years and I've discovered that similar to the satisfaction of knowing you have been run out of better bars or towns than where you find yourself now (up to the neck in trouble?) is knowing that you've been becalmed in places un-excelled in their ability to awaken an appreciation of what is often an unpleasant or at best an uncomfortable experience. I should and usually do remember my good experiences, but likewise I never forget my bad ones.

A few years ago while becalmed in the Anegada channel, I was boarded and searched by the Coast Guard who, finding no violations aboard my ship, steamed over the horizon looking for more exciting quarry. Dawn found me not far from the same position as I watched the approaching bow-wave of the same cutter, which felt obligated to search again, being unable to understand that with still no wind, I was still becalmed, and again fishing deep. They disappeared into the south and the mid-morning breeze allowed me to continue on to Jost Van Dyke, and prevented me from being able to greet on a first name basis the crew of the cutter who I assume would have boarded me a third time!

I once went on a sunset sail near Isla Mujeres, Mexico with a cruising friend and two Dutch airline stewardesses who were scheduled to fly out the next morning. After the fourth day of absolute flat calm, the two ladies were suffering from extreme anxiety coupled with an intense inability to appreciate the natural wonder of the Gulf Stream's ability to carry us North while we floated on a flat and windless sea. They were unable to derive any pleasure from the sight of schools of large Barracudas that lingered in tiers below us or to properly applaud the acrobatic display given to us by a pod of Orca. Even if they had been interested they probably would have attempted to throw the captain to these visiting 'killer-whales'. They were very happy to return to Mexico but to date I have not yet received any cards or even a note of appreciation. Some things are just not nice to think about no matter how well we remember them.

Most things experienced under a regimen of enforced solitude and sensory deprivation affect us deeply, as evidenced by the statistics concerning the relative degree of neurosis in different working fields. Fully 12% of sailors suffer some form of neuroses making sailing one of the most dangerous/hazardous of careers. Fortunately however this allows the sailor an excuse, other than Rum, to appear or act a bit 'mad' to his land bound contemporaries Oft-times it is better to appear 'mad' than to actually 'make a stake' in an unwelcoming climate. Better perhaps to choke back ones "gall" and assume the pained expression of the chronic dyspepsic and as Thoreau said "to live ones' life in quiet desperation", join the legions of those assassins of dreams and ideals who seem to spend their lives dismantling mountains, assembling plains, confusing good intentions with bad laws unwilling and unable to acknowledge any experience that differs from 'peer' standards. It is one thing to decry 'nuclear or biohazard' production and be outraged by any atrocity against life and quite another thing to actually write that letter to your government representative or actually speak out to those same peers.

I've decided to grab a few of these bullish chimeras by the horns possibly making a few enemies, probably a few 'allies' and maybe a friend or two, but mostly for my own sake. To ease that dull ache below my right ribs that says 'my gall is up'. I'm going to talk about things that are often unpleasant...like killing sea-turtles in the Grenadines for their eggs and slaughtering them before even killing them...about the 200 or more pilot whales and hundreds more porpoises killed yearly in the Caribbean and just what does the 'Marine-Fat' source label really mean on many of the Antillean produced margarines.

Soon we will all be knee-deep in plastic soda bottles and that though drift nets have been internationally banned since 1992 a twenty kilometer long section of a 50 foot 'wall of death' was recently found unattended south of Grenada. I'm going to talk about the 'throw-away' world of plastics, about Asian fishing fleets operating in these islands and about charter yachts with four heads, twenty four hour a day generators, video libraries, jet skis and air conditioning. Roger Fothergill of Tern IV once said to me, "its just a dam shame when the specific gravity of the ships batteries is more important to guests and crew than the seaworthiness of the hull, bottom or rig!" These are not pleasant things to discuss, they are not even nice to acknowledge but they must be acknowledged for unlike the helpless plight of a becalmed sailing ship a lot of these issues might be resolved or at least better understood if people are willing to discuss their occurrence, their differences and reflect upon how they affect our lives.

In the Middle Ages there was a widely discussed yet never fully resolved 'conundrum' that held the attention of both the scientists and the philosophers. 'If a dead fish is put in a vessel full of water the vessel will overflow; but, if a live fish is put in the same vessel it will not overflow'

Our curiosity leads us to conjecture on why this is so. But, when we do not further investigate we become less like our distant cousins the whale but more like ostriches with our heads in the sand. Our situation will not be resolved. If we cease to take notice, make comment and use the magic of our lives to protect and preserve the beauty that surrounds us, of which we are all "heirs".

BILGE WATER, WATER SPOUTS, & TIGHT SPOTS

Nice and breezy in the Mermaid' these days; I've torn out three deck beams and a few deck planks and about 15 feet of sheer clamp, so it's gotten mighty easy to observe the outside weather conditions without leaving the cabin. Unfortunately, it also allows quite a bit of weather to enter the cabin, causing the bilge water to be measured in feet and the pumping to be measured in long minutes. Oft-times I return from a land expedition, glance into the bilge, and wonder which side of the boat it came in from top or bottom, fresh or salt. It looks the same, a bit clear maybe, but still nasty. So I spit in it.

Yeah, I spit in the bilge. If the saliva breaks up, it means it is saltwater and the boat has a leak and might be sinking, but if it just sits there like a blob of toothpaste in the sink it means the water tanks have failed and leaked or, as in my case that the deck is gone and it has rained. A handy trick, especially if there is any oil floating on the surface. Of course, there are people who ask for volunteers to have a sip or taste it themselves. Full bilges make it tougher to test as frightened people can't spit you know.

I found myself in a bit of a tight spot a few weeks ago and lost my ability to spit. While sailing with a lady friend enroute to Anguilla, wearing only smiles and sombreros, we became becalmed on the very edge of some nasty weather to the north. My friend asked me what the "funny" weather to south was, and that's when I lost my color (she said), the spit dried up, my eyes got bigger, and other parts of me got smaller (she said).

It was a newly formed waterspout not 100 yards away heading directly towards Mermaid. I covered the 40-odd feet to the foredeck in record time and dumped sail I didn't "scandalize the mains'l." I dropped everything and let the halyards run as we were hit by over 100 knots of wind and laid on our beam ends. The number two dinghy was washed overboard and everything in it and on deck disappeared. The waterspout lasted only 15-20 seconds and just walked, or twisted, its way toward the west. Except for what was washed away, we suffered no breakage, except that the strain opened the seams a bit, hence the salty bilge. Fishermen in Anguilla advised me to always keep a cutlass at the wheel and slash at the approaching whirlwind, but at the time I was sailing with the Mescalero Apache Girl who liked tequila, so I kept all the knives hidden.

Most people were amazed to hear of our firsthand encounter. My old-time sailing friend and editor Geoff Smith was quite upset to hear from a friend that yes, you can get hit by a waterspout. He had conveniently convinced himself that it just didn't happen and was consequently disturbed to have his theory squashed!

Years earlier, on Isla Mujeres in Mexico, shipmate Dave Goldhill and I, in company with another "madman," jogged on a parallel course to a 'spout' as it crossed the island. The upwelling of water was displaced by the upwelling of laundry garbage cans, sheet metal, and coconuts. As it re-crossed water in the anchorage it knocked over an anchored 40-foot sloop while sucking everything out the open ports and hatches. Mermaid anchored 100 yards away was untouched except for a ½ inch layer of sand upon her decks!

Later in the evening on the day of our encounter near Anguilla, we were visiting a neighboring yacht and were telling the English singlehander of our experience. He looked at us as if we were crazy or drunk or just plain making up sea stories at his expense. He did not believe in waterspouts until we turned his attention to the west where just beyond Anguilitta and clearly visible we watched THREE SEPARATE

SPOUTS form and move off into the channel like giant snakes charmed by some celestial flute, hypnotic, sinuous, and deadly.

HIDE AND SEEK OR
SEARCH AND RESCUE

Mermaid is sitting comfortably to a mooring here in Mt. Hartmans' Bay on the south coast of the 'big-island'—Grenada. Its' taken a bit of getting used to 'Big-Islands', and I haven't quite adjusted to Jet-Airlines passing directly overhead in departing Pt. Salines International Airport. Last month it was helicopters. The U.S. Marines allowed its' reservists to pick up some needed flight time and presumably, the 'war-on-drugs' resulted in thousands of marijuana plant casualties. They pulled out last week—back to Georgia and the sound of the departing C-5 Transport was the decibel equivalent of being between GM 6-71's in the hold of a shrimper!

Its' normal Airlines Schedules now—almost quiet. There is very little music here however, 'cept for the Steel Band in Secret Harbour and last week, the Carriacou band brought some rhythm to Prickly Bay. They have a female lead singer who is so good that people stop dancing and just stand around listening!

In Carriacou, there is always music: Blocko, Disco or the combined volumes of a hundred radios tuned to106 FM and recently I listened to the same Whitney Houston album for three days after Fitzroy left town leaving the volume up and the auto reverse on. So it was nice to hear the down-home band "NO-I.D." that I had heard practicing all summer. I was eager to un-wind. The boat had just been launched after a week on the hard. I had gotten off of a reef only a week earlier. I love the tropics, but oft-times tropical weather leaves much to be desired for the short-handed engineless cruiser. Eight hours out from Carriacou found Mermaid becalmed in the lee of Pt. Saline. The meeting of ocean tide and still water—unsettled I did circles with the other float-sam till a light breeze tempted me to attempt the lay of Prickly Bay. I got close, but it grew dark and once again calm—drawing Mermaid towardsthe deeper water near shore. With no steerage and land much too close, I anchored on a drifting reach, gybed and 'CRUNCH"! I was aground, but gently.

The kedge I dropped held so I re-hoisted the mains'l and sat softly by the halyards, gently crushing coral and not so gently removing ten feet of my worm shoe. I grabbed three 37mm red parachute flares, one failed but the other two lighted the entire Medical School Campus at True Blue while attracting the attention of customers at the Tiki Bar and Restaurant in Prickly Bay. Five people at the bar saw the flares and at least three aboard yachts alerted the Coast Guard who were of the opinion that the flares were 'too near the shore' to mean emergency, probably only a prank! Presumably they investigated the next morning, but with a light breeze Mermaid had OFF to sea, into the south and deep water, to drift becalmed again, 48 miles into the West. Locating my Venezuelan charts became top priority. A school of Dorado had chosen my home as their 'tree-fort' and with a piece of sun cured tuna I captured six, which I filleted, salted and put out to dry. For three days there was not a breath of wind or a sound to be heard. I dove on the hull and once again with my trusty very rusty T-50 staple gun covered the gouges with lead. A SW wind on the fourth day gave me a perfect Easting reach and soon I was safely anchored in Prickly Bay—half mile from where I had run-aground and to my astonishment only a quarter mile from the Coast Guard Base! I hadn't gotten on the VHF, assuming the C.G. were in St. Georges. I preferred to use the electric pump and launch rockets while doing my best to sail away doing as little damage as possible.

For two hours I crushed coral. I surrendered the anchor to fate it had done its job, but I wondered about the Coast Guard. As a fisher-man I can appreciate access to ice, fuel and water most of which is sup-plied by private business on Petit Martinique but I would like to see the Fisheries agency in Windward re-opened. Instead, the Grenadians are getting a new Coast Guard Bases, the function of which is presumably to protect the Marine Interests of the people and the nation. The interests of the people are maintaining independence, protecting their freedom and surviving at sea. For the protein and the prestige supplied by a seafaring life style the sea takes it's toll. A young fisherman of Windward was lost presumed drowned after his small fishing vessel was found dismasted and adrift west of Carriacou. Last week, another half-sunk drifting vessel was found west of St. Georges. Is not, or should not 'Rescue' be a result of 'Search'? Is not search and rescue the primary duty of the Coast Guard?

In the British Coast Guards every officer is a Fisheries Officer (Fact) and perhaps the most picturesque of his duties is to take charge of the "Fish-Royal"—the sturgeon, whale, porpoise and dolphin that may happen, as it were, to swim within his Ken, and probably the most peculiar form of coast-watching is carried out on the Sussex coast at Winchelsea. For five centuries there has been a job known as the "look-out". The French Fleet had invaded here and sacked the town and ever since the look-out makes a twice daily scan of the horizon. If the Coast-Guards consider themselves more of a police unit than a service of the people, then it becomes the role of the people to take-care and 'watch out' for each other.

I was enlightened to this situation by the marine pilots who implied that had my grounding been 'drug-related', I would have had more help than I needed. But I'm not really surprised. I'm still upset about the Red-Right-Returning controversy.

Twenty five years ago all the islands (except U.S. territories) conformed to the English and International Marine law under which a vessel 'returning' is one returning-to-sea atotally different approach than the return-to-harbor attitude presently being adopted to mimic the U.S. laws. Remember what they tell the Bare Boat charters in St. Thomas? "Always keep the land in sight and never, ever, sail at night", in which case we wouldn't need a coast guard, just a good 'look out'.

FRIDAY THE THIRTEENTH

Friends of mine just put to sea enroute to Sint Maarten, and it was not until the lingering tone of my conch shell salute had faded into the brisk vent-noell that I realized it was Friday, and Friday the 13th as well. I'm not generally a superstitious sort of guy but I silently, wished them a safe voyage, for most sailors know that Friday, "Freya's Day", has always been regarded as a bad day to either begin the construction of a ship, to launch a ship or to go to sea.

This ancient custom stems from the association of Friday with Freya—the Norse goddess of love and beauty, who was also leader of the Valkryies, who rode onto the battlefield to claim the dead. This may seem strange, but to the Norse was a natural and fitting a duty for the goddess of love. "There is a place called Folkvang, and there Freyia is in charge of allotting seats in the hall. Half the slain she chooses each day, and half has Odin."

In the nineteenth century, the British Navy tried to dispel this superstition and the keel of a new ship was laid on Friday, she was named HMS Friday, launched on a Friday and finally went to sea on a Friday. The Captains name was Friday. Neither the ship nor her crew were ever heard of again.

Thursday, on the other hand, is an especially good day to begin a ship or to commence a voyage, for Thursday is "Thor's Day", the thunder god and strongest of the Aesir. One should however avoid beginning a voyage on the first Monday in April—the day Cain slew his brother, Abel; the second Monday in August—the day Sodom and Gomorrah were destroyed and December 31st—the day that Judas Iscariot hanged himself from an Elder Tree on ground that became the first potters' field. (The same Elder tree that was sacred to Freya and chosen as her abode because of its beneficial qualities). Later, in Medieval Europe, the Elder gained its bad reputation and became associated with evil and witches.

It was a windy Friday, however, so my friends probably had their hands full, taking their old gaffer across Anegada Channel, so probably did not have time or opportunity to shave or trim their hair at sea, and as hair is a votive offering to Persephone, queen of the lower world, Neptune would have become jealous indeed of offerings to another god made in his kingdom.

RIGHTS OF PASSAGE

I was having the strangest dream. It had to be a dream because the sound "beep-beep" is not something often heard upon the high sea. It was like that little Nash Rambler trying to pass the larger Cadillac, "beep-beep". I had gone below at dawn to catch a few "Z's" and just let the Mermaid slip along on steady course of WNW. She hadn't wavered 10 degrees all night, and with Virgin Gorda just now visible off the starboard bow.

I slipped into "dreams-ville" for a few hours. But the "beep-beep" wouldn't go away, maybe this is not a dream. Nope, not a dream, for just off my quarter is a 110-foot long U.S. Coast Guard cutter. Maybe they tried to call me on the VHF, but mine is not normally switched 'on' because, except for emergency or "import" communications, I'd rather save the electricity for running lights or have available power should I need a pump or maybe good ole "rock'n'roll" during the dark and lonely pre-dawn watch.

Five 'coasties' in an inflatable came alongside, and after I volunteered the information that I was not armed, I gave them permission to board me. They couldn't really understand what I was doing out there and found it hard to believe that I was alone, and yes, I'd been asleep, and of course I knew about "Hurricane Chris", but it was hundreds of miles to the East. None of these fellas had ever been in Simpson Bay Lagoon surrounded by hundreds of hastily-abandoned bare-boats, so they were unable to appreciate the beauty of the Anegada Passage on a comfortable reach. No matter what "Chris" did, in the next few days I would either be safely tied in the mangroves of Hurricane Hole or running South with cracked sheets.

Two Coastguardsmen, err, two Coastguards people, were searching the ship for whatever they search for, and two engaged the 'crew' of Mermaid in chit-chat. When it came to filling in the blank space on the boarding form as to 'make of vessel', we decided "homemade" was the obvious choice, and now I've been officially designated with engine as they entered my 30-year old British Seagull as ships power!

By 1030 that morning, the cutter Okracoke was hull down to the southwest and Mermaid continued steering herself towards St. John. Time now for a pot of tea and maybe spend an hour with a good book. Suddenly it starts all over again, not a little "beep-beep", no sir this was a full-roaring ships' horn giving the 5-blast International danger signal. Two miles off my port beam is a ship, so I look around to see who is in trouble. There is no shipping visible but me and him, and I'm okay, no trouble here, except that my tea is getting cold. Another 5 shattering blasts as the ship now seems intent upon ramming the Mermaid. On VHF/16 I contact the approaching ship and inquire as to his intentions. I am told in nouncertain terms to "get out of his way!" Well, like I said, I've been on the same course now for almost 20 hours with a preventer on the 26 foot-long boom running dead down wind, and now I've got to "get out of the way"?

The M/S Oyster now 800 yards away seems fully ready to run me over, and her captain continued his VHF demands (on Channel #16) saying that I had deliberately cut across his bow! Well, at 5 knots I don't do much "cutting", and I try to explain that as a sailing ship in broad daylight might it not be best for me to maintain course and speed? I return to the deck grabbing my 37 mm rockets.

My eyes have never been very good, but now I can read the ships' name clearly and realize that the superstructure is bright red and that the Oyster is a 250 foot Propane Carrier! OOPS; best put the flares aside, but I'm still not going any faster. I have removed the preventer and pulled the fishing line in as the ship passes within 50 yards at over 15 knots. From below the VHF comes alive with some very colorful Venezuelan English cursing me in the roundest terms.

On days like that I'd like to be on a submarine, no horns, no "beep-beep", just the roaring klaxon as I dive-dive. Maybe I'll just paint Mermaid red, carry a few extra propane bottles and then I too can disregard all "Rules of the Road".

International Collision Regulations
Rule #15 Crossing Situation
"When two vessels are crossing so as to involve risk of collision, the vessel which has the other on her own starboard side shall keep out of the way and avoid crossing ahead of the other vessel."

SON OF A GUN

The Navy and Coast Guard are pretty busy these days with all the 'boat people'. That's not only me but most of you and all the 'livea-boards' from Simpson Bay to Sausalito—the established refugees. The new wave of Haitian and Cuban 'boat people' is a tsunami of human-ity that tests the limitations and virtues of the ships and crews.

More than 30% of the 'raft people' are women and children, and many children have been born aboard the patrolling ships, which do carry both men and women as crew and officers. a good opportunity for working together and observing first hand the joys and sufferings of those who 'go to sea' looking for chance at a new life. I wonder if the children born aboard these ships earn the right to call themselves 'son of a gun'?

Originally this was a complimentary term meaning a seaman born at sea. It derived from the period when wives 'other ladies of the port' lived aboard in harbour, and even occasionally at sea. Those born on the gun deck were entered as 'Son of a Gun'. In 1792, while undergo-ing a refit at Spithead, the Royal George capsized in one of the most unusual in harbour catastrophes of the British navy. Over 1000 people were drowned—and more than 300 were women!

This was the era that gave us the expression 'show a leg' or 'shake a leg'. As the master at Arms patrolled the gun deck, with his 'Stonnicky' rousing the crew, they were ordered to 'show a leg'. If the leg was hairy the hammock was cut down, if it was smooth and feminine them the occupant was left in peace, undisturbed!

In February of 1994, the US Navy reached a milestone of sorts—for the first time in its history a sailor gave birth aboard a Navy Warship. I don't doubt the entire crew toasted that 'Son of a Gun' all around.

When I was in the Navy I served aboard an AKA, Attack Cargo Auxiliary. We had our heliport on the stern, a few old five inchers, many 20mm antiaircraft batteries and a largish hospital where I served as corpsman. The sound of the 'choppers' usually meant work for the hospital and not infrequently were we able to give medical aid and succor to entire families, occasionally assisting with child birth. I found peace in knowing that the ship was well supplied with every commodity and that the crew were well trained. I sincerely hope that the Coast Guard and Navy crews of today, on patrol in the Caribbean, look upon their mission as an opportunity to give aid and to better understand themselves, their duties, 'boat people' and all the rest.

THE SHOT HEARD ROUND
THE WORLD

Everyone seems to know the story of the first salute to the American flag from Fort Orange and its long-term repercussions to both the Dutch (England ultimately declared war on Holland) and the multitudes of free-traders who with the capture of St. Eustatia by Rodne in 1781 were the last to see the island in its economic glory. On 16 November 1776, the privateer Andrew Doria, flying American colors entered the port, seized an English vessel from under the guns of the Dutch fort, saluted with 11 guns, made off with its prize, and received a nine-gun salute back. Heady stuff! Especially within sight of other British merchant vessels and warships. Statia was a busy place and over 3,200 ships cleared in a 13-month period between 1778 and 1779.

When Rodney returned, "to scourge them", on 3 February 1791 after the declaration of war with Holland, he effectively broke the economic back of St. Eustatia, and she has never recovered her former grandeur.

The ironic twist of this story is that the bulk of the captured stores ultimately were supplied to the Americans at a 50-percent reduction of what probably would have been paid to the Dutch. For within days of Rodney's departure, a handful of French under the Marquis de Boville recaptured the island with three frigates and 400 men. The Marquis dressed his troops in red coats and was able to capture an entire division of British, who were taking their exercise on a field. The English governor, returning from his morning ride, was likewise captured. The French estimated their spoils at over 2 million livres and gallantly returned 13,000 livres to the English governor, who was soon to have need of it as he was subsequently court-martialed and cashiered.

Rodney's fleet meanwhile was plundered by French warships and later suffered losses in a hurricane. The cargoes had now changed hands three times and would soon be delivered to the American rebels. So, in fact, Rodney's act actually aided the American side but ruined Statia as a freeport. The war would soon be over on the American colonies, but England and Holland fought for two more years. A nice historical tale. There is a flaw, however, Statia, which suffered so much, was not in fact the scene of that first salute. The actual first salute was not by the Dutch, BUT BY THE DANES.

On 25 October 1776, an unidentified schooner in Frederiksted Roads St. Croix, loaded a cargo of gunpowder, made sail, and after hoisting the American colors saluted the fort with 11 guns asmuch as to say thank you and the officer in command of the fort ordered the salute returned. An onlooker, a Mr. Kelly, two days later put his indignation on paper to British Vice Admiral Young in Antigua. "My astonishment was great to find such a commerce countenanced by government here. The vessel went out under American colors, saluted the fort, and had the compliment returned as if she had been an English or Danish ship." From the British point of view, this act was an outrage and an "insult to the British flag." Letters flew between the naval chief of the Windward and Governor-General Claussen of St. Croix, and the English representative in Copenhagen protested that war materials were clearing the harbors of all three Danish islands.

The Danes took the view that this was off-shore trading, which it was, and hadn't Ben Franklin just recently backed the Continental Congress in a resolution which permitted all vessels carrying war goods to enter American waters and export American products of equal value? What better incentive to trade with the colonials from transshipment points in the Caribbean.

Frederiksted and Statia soon became the busiest smuggling ports in the entire New World. St. Croix was suddenly rivaling Jamaica and

Barbados as the most important sugar-producing island in the West Indies. In 1764 the Danish crown had liberalized the trading laws, giving their possessions in the Caribbean freeport status. This allowed the Virgin Islands to "not smuggle" to the Dutch island, for now the new laws put all the Danish islands at the same advantage. The trade prospered. Many a war-weary American soldier had little but a ration of rum, dispensed from one of Boston's 40 distilleries, to get him through the cold winter nights. Rum made from golden Cruzan muscovado sugar. Molasses, wrote John Adams, played an essential part in American independence

And it was on St. Croix that Rachel Faucet Lavien married a naturalized Dane from whom she fled to marry the young Scot James Hamilton of Nevis, to return two years later to be with her Cruzan relatives. Her son, Alexander Hamilton, spent his youth and apprenticed as a young man within the thriving St. Croix freeport economic system.

Perhaps it was young Hamilton's experiences here, his observations of privateering, piracy, slave trading, and smuggling, which later prompted him as the first Secretary of the Treasury to establish the US Coast Guard. The Dutch had been involved for a longer time however, and with the British declaration of war the Danish ports became the only neutral spots to all those homeless and technically stateless pirates, privateers, and roving merchants now barred from the Dutch island. Holland was at war, but Danemark had managed to protect its privileged neutrality.

The Danish fort need not have saluted that unknown American schooner, but it did. Perhaps the young Danish officer in charge was afraid of repeating his predecessors' mistake when, in April of 1776, the British sloop-of-war Hind under Captain Byrnne cruised the roadsted of Frederiksted without showing colors or saluting the fort and searched several ships at anchor, finally sweeping out to sea carrying an unidentified brigantine as a prize of war. On that day the cannon had remained silent and that Danish officer was court martialed. On October of 1776, the Danes were operating 245 vessels of 80 to 120 tons burden, but with the success of Washington's army at Yorktown and the ending of the French-English-Dutch American hostilities, the number rapidly fell to below 90.

In 1917 these islands became US territory for $325 per acre whereas Secretary of State Seward's purchase of Alaska several decades earlier had cost the Americans $.07 per acre, and the canal zone so conveniently made available within the new nation of Panama was scooped by Teddy Roosevelt for $27 per acre. Footnotes to history.

Ironic though, today Statia is still Dutch, whereas the island that had been designated the Danish capital of the West Indies in 1755 and had been Carib, Spanish, French, English and been administered by the Knights of Malta, the Danish West Indian Company, and finally the Danish crown was to become a United States territory and fly the same flag she, "First in the World," had saluted in October of 1776, in St. Croix's own shot,' Heard round the world.

TO SEE OR NOT TUNA SEE

There is no reason why you should believe any of what I am now going to tell you. Even the photos I took of the event do not 'prove' a thing. They are only photos. No one but myself knows for certain that they were not produced in some Hollywood studio where many people believed Neil Armstrong took his "great leap for mankind". I ask you to believe me even though when it was happening, I did not correctly identify what I was watching happen. "Seeing is Believing" the popular expression goes, but as Santayana once pointed out, humans are better at believing than at seeing. The map is not the terrain.

I believed I was seeing a black dog being very unwillingly washed in the sea by two young Anguillan boys. The people seated with me at 'Johnnos' in Sandy Ground, Anguilla…at the same table even, believed they saw two boys struggling with a sea-turtle. (At least we got the same numbers.) We all believed what we saw except that the 'dog' or 'turtle' was beating the crap out of the boys who now seemed to be stabbing it with a knife. We were so confused that we left 3 cold beers and as many rum'n cokes on the bench and went to investigate.

It wasn't a dog or a turtle, but they certainly were struggling, and so far it was a tie. Both boys and a large tunafish were struggling and were equally splattered with blood and sand. I grabbed a 6-foot length of 2 x 4 and with the practiced swing of a high seas fisherman "quieted" the tuna. The fish was about the same girth as either of the boys, weighed 44 pounds and measured 45 inches. It apparently had been chasing lunch among a large shoal of bait fish when it ran itself aground where 'Lex' Marlon Richardson and Jaudi Hughes (both 9 years old) did not for one second hesitate to jump on it and commence to wrestle it up the beach.

Hard to believe, but over 8 people watched it happen, and we all saw a different thing. What we imagined was happening was more real to us than what Lex and Jaudi were actually doing. So don't under-rate the kids these days and let's not so readily convince ourselves that any of us knows the whole truth. Remember, it's impossible to get through the keyhole with the key in your hand.

CHANGING PLANS AND PLANNING CHANGES

It was supposed to have been an overnight fishing trip. Celebrate the full moon offshore. Enjoy the lights of the Virgin Islands from the perspective of the 100-fathom curve south of St. John. Cruise the seamount or "hump" with deep baits and maybe entice a yellowfin tuna to a sushi feast we would gladly give in its honor, like the "Walrus and the Carpenter". Crew were engaged for "the overnighter" and just in case, the ship's offshore water bottles were filled at the preposterous price of 70 US cents a gallon—whew! Ballyhoo and sprat baits were put aboard and before noon we were off, port tack heading southeast at 4 knots. A bit too fast for deep fishing, but maybe we can attract a wahoo along the edge, so back on a northbound starboard tack and a STRIKE, just south of Santa Monica Rock. The line runs, a good fish but…oops, not a good fish is a 30-pound king mackerel when caught along this coast. A man can't give a kingfish away up here and in the Virgins nobody but a fool eats barracuda or any of the canine-toothed snappers. Ciguatera poisoning is a very real fact of life (or death) in the areas affected.

Statistics show that fully 15 percent of those affected die of the cumulative affects unless they seek attention at a hospital equipped to deal with the loss of fluid and toxic shock. For many years there appeared to be a marked prevalence of ciguatera poisoning in the US and French territories. Did this tendency for the specific bloom of the specific blue-green algae causing the syndrome arise because of some hi-tech chemical spill, or perhaps developmental run-off or maybe uncontrolled dredging, or bottom paint from cruising sailboats leaching into the sea? Well no. Actually only the French and .US medical personnel did adequate pathology on both the suspected fish and the sufferer to determine the specific syndrome and to pin-point the particular organism. By any name ciguatera poisoning is not a nice experience particularly when 200 miles offshore. A biochemist at the University of Hawaii has developed a dip-stick type test kit which should soon be available for shipboard use, but nevertheless I for one will continue to be pretty careful what fish I eat once I'm north of Guadeloupe.

But now I'm over again on port tack so as not to run afoul of Anegada with its White Horse Reef, and once again Mermaid's bowsprit points our way to a civilized Carriacou rum shop. I have recently acquired a puppy, a "schipperke/esquimaux" and was told that the seventh week is the most important period for bonding to occur, for an imprint to be burned into the consciousness of the animal bonding it to its pack or master, or in this case the ship because we spent that entire week at sea and the dog is now bonded to a rolling deck, salt spray and fresh buttergarlic poached wahoo and dorado.

The dog is of a breed that is alleged to bark when lights or land appear, he remained silent that entire week but seemed a little stressed, as did the rest of the crew, when a Royal Navy helicopter hovered some 50 meters away. They were obviously looking for some identification, so I reached for the ships' life-ring inscribed thereon with the ships' name and homeport, and now encircling the captain's face and waving the puppy, kinda like Buster Brown and his buddy Tiger in their shoe. We had our pictures taken and a "thumbs-up" wig-wag as they roared into the east where next day we met up with a. frigate and attendant choppers.

I've named the pup Winger as in 18th century sailing slang for a shore-going companion, sidekick or protege. In consideration of my swimming habits (often and distant}, my friend advised that the water-loving pup should swim with me and if a shark were to appear, the dogmeat would hopefully be the more appealing fare. Tough on the dog but probably good for the swimmer. My friend liked the ring of the name "Sharkbait", but being the sensitive sort I refrained and stuck with Winger although I might on occasion refer to my little sidekick as Chum.

On the third or fourth day out the crew realized this was not the typical overnight fishing trip, although daily the fishing improved! Their plans had to be changed, which really shouldn't be too difficult for someone with a schedule or a time frame. People with a program are actually better able to indulge in the stress-releasing exercise of Changing Plans, whereas after about the fifth day Planning Changes became the dynamic, the pursuit and name of the game. The captain's planning change to stay strapped down on the port tack out onto the broad blue back of the Caribbean rather than adhere to the plan and tack back to the green, coral-ringed shallows of Sir Francis Drake's Channel, had demanded a re-evaluation of their ability to meet their pre-departure schedule. Heading offshore fully provisioned with not a penny aboard seemed the sensible thing to do, cash has often been called the fuel of change and with enough of this fuel one might realistically make a plan, but offshore it is best to have no particular plan, especially with a 20-ton engineless gaff cutter. It still amazes me how many people on how many near-perfect boats (requiring full-time servicing and often full-time jobs) almost' always change their plans and rarely go anywhere (if going anywhere was ever part of their plan).

As outlined in "Teja's Law of Gnostic Ecology" (see Compass April 1998 issue) life aboard Float Street and Mermaid demands a Gnostic awareness of the inherent propriety of planning on changes to occur which is just a fancy way of saying 'shit happens' and adopting a willingness to be resilient and accept the fact that sometimes the ship or the weather or the sea or the whim are actually better teachers than any clock or calendar. I had advised the crew to bring their passports and promised them that within 3 days we would "be somewhere" and thanks to the miracle of the Global Positioning System I was able to tell them where we were to within 15 meters! They had had a plan, a schedule, and a fantasy. Now they had a precise position, two miles of seawater, and the ship still beneath their feet.

Dawn of the seventh day and the Grenadines are looking 'sweet-sweet' Plans change here, and time is more than a clock thrown towards the sun; we wait for changes, accept them, embrace them, and the waiting is always full.

SCARLETT, THE SPACE STATION AND "VITRUVIAN MAN 1492"

It is amazing how little the ocean has changed and how very much the navigational equipment available to me has, and that in only 33 years of living aboard. It was only a thousand years or so ago that a magnetized piece of iron on a cork in a bowl of water was acknowledged to be an important directional aid and we've all heard how Mr. Harrison's Clock allowed the art of astral-navigation to become the relatively exact science it is. The octant and sextant are centuries old and knowledge of the celestial sphere with its stars and wandering planets has been understood, mapped and utilized by desert travelers in Egypt and the Sahara for millennium.

In my lifetime I have witnessed the development and widespread use of loran, radar, sat-nav., depth sounders, and I am presently in awe of that super toy of the American defense department-the GPS. We can know our position to within a few meters and the depth beneath us to a few feet but our sense of 'inter-connectedness" has somehow been undermined if not totally lost. Only a few people (and most of them astrologers) have any knowledge of the celestial sphere and our particular relation to it, from within it. We are 'here' and the sky is 'there'.

Degrees of position are now measured to three decimal places on our computer defined position but fewer and fewer people have any understanding of altitudes, azimuths, trigonometry or any of the other applications of the 'natural sciences' once so essential to any blue-water sailor. There was a time (not so long ago) when a seaman's skill with a sextant and a plotting sheet were the primary indicators of his trade and his professionalism.

On Christmas Eve of 2001, residents of the eastern Caribbean were treated with a rare double nights' sighting (at sunset) of the International Space Station passing overhead and the analogy of "Santa's sled" came easily to mind. I have a young friend, 6 year old Scarlett, who became quite excited when told that yes, this year; we would be able to see Santa's sled as it passes by! How to explain to Scarlett about angles, and altitudes and angular differences as it passed by in just over 3 minutes? She would not understand a sextant and it is not an efficient tool in the dark in the hands of a 6 year old when looking for something moving so fast. Her dad had a GPS (and a spare), so they knew where they were but it was of no help in finding a passing celestial body.

We knew that the station was expected to rise in the N at 1829 on the 24 of Dec. and to pass approximately 35 degrees above the eastern horizon traveling SW, and we knew that on 25 Dec. it would rise in the NW and travel to the S perhaps reaching an altitude of 50 degrees.

The space station remains in orbit because it is traveling at just a little less than escape velocity (17,500mph) which means that it completes one full orbit every one and one-half hours, (16 orbits a day!) Because it is a passive light source, only reflecting the suns' light, it is only visible at dawn and at sunset, and then for only a few minutes. Being of the old school (a celestial navigator) I was able to quickly distinguish the station from the known stars and planets and then try to point it out to Scarlet, who saw it and was quite pleased. She wondered only where it would land! My attempt "to explain" astronomy to a 6 year old gave me much food for thought.

A week earlier I was having coffee aboard a Swiss yacht when the Captain asked me what I thought to be the angular height or "altitude" of the highest peak visible to us. His estimate was almost 15 degrees off of mine which was only 1 degree from fact. I was not carrying my sextant or borrow his, but I applied a lesson taught in the 15th century by of all things-a painter! This painter was also the unexcelled anatomist, engineer, inventor and visionary of the Renaissance and I refer to the painting "The proportions of Man" by Leonardo daVinci. With this painting daVinci illustrated the fact that all normally proportioned people regardless of age, sex, race, or size maintain the same proportions relative to a circle. That is to say: there are 18 spans, or 36 hands, or 180 fingers in a circle. If I or you or your child stands with our right arms extended and hand maximally spread, this span when viewed with the left eye is 20 degrees of a circle. Our hand (4 fingers in a fist) is 10 degrees and the width of our extended index finger is 2 degrees. If we extend our left arms and close our left eye the proportion remains the same. If I see an object in the sky or peak of a distant hill or the top of a tree and it is 1 span, 1 fist and 2 fingers high, its' altitude is 34 degrees, (20 plus 10 plus 4). Similarly if two mountains on separate islands are separated by one span and one finger the horizontal angle is approximately 22 degrees. If I know the height of these objects (from a chart) I can easily compute a near distance off using My Bowditch or Nautical almanac. If I decide to be more precise and use my sextant, having an approximate altitude allows me to 'pre-set' my instrument.

If we understand the circle and the earth and the celestial sphere to have 360 degrees and a day to be 24 hours long we can see that there are 15 degrees of rotation per hour or 1 degree every 4 minutes. Therefore if we can identify any fixed object in the sky, the sun, a star or a planet we can use daVincis' "proportions of Man" and our extended arm and hand to get a fairly accurate estimate of it's altitude to measure the passage of time or to pre-set our sextants.

One span is 20 degrees and is therefore 80 minutes of time, one hand is 10 degrees or 40 minutes of time and one finger is 2 degrees or 8 minutes of time. With theses 'tools' we can quite easily compute the passage of time and quite easily differentiate the 12 separate houses of the zodiac, all of which lie within the plane of the ecliptic and equal approximately 30 degrees. If we measure the altitude of the setting sun by this method we can easily determine the time till 'touchdown' with our 2 degree or 8 minutes of time width fingers.

In this day and age the prudent navigator is advised to make use of all information available for the safe navigation and passage of his/her vessel and this includes all the electronics available when available but very often it is the power supply which fails and not the equipment. The United States Defense Department might de-regulate the GPS system at any time. Not everyone has back-up radar or Loran, so do not be to quick to put away the more traditional tools, and these include the "proportions of man", Scarletts' hand, the space station and of course, Santa Claus.

HURRICANE SEASON COMES AGAIN AND AGAIN AND…

It's time again. 'That' time again, 'H' season, the 'H' word, the Carib God of Wind—HURACAN; not to be spoken, lest summoned. And when he/she arrives we feel our unworthiness, are aware of our frail glory and are never totally prepared or ever really ready to do it again. We try to be prepared and ready, but how to prepare for the indescribable power that is HURACAN? How are we ever ready for a force we cannot comprehend? So what to do? Short of spending summers in Montana or the Czech Republic, or filling the boat with dirt and starting a home nursery or bar below decks, there's not much we can do, but it helps a bit to know what to expect.

This is my 33rd season in the Tropics. I have weathered storms from Grenada to The Virgins, to the Yucatan Coast and Florida. The only good news is that with modern weather broadcasting we can at least monitor a storm's track, and by applying a ~6th century mariner's rule named Buys Ballots' Law we can better predict the conditions we ought to expect as a storm approaches.

Buys Ballots' Law states that an observer in the Northern Hemisphere facing the wind will have the center of low pressure approximately 100 to 110 degrees to his right side, somewhat behind him; and the center of high pressure toward his left and somewhat in front.

In the Northern Hemisphere, if the observer points his/her left hand, palm down into the wind and extends the thumb maximally, the center of the low is in the angle and direction of the thumb. This low indicates the storm's center and we can then predict the direction of the expected wind and seek the best anchorage within reach, or we can run.

Normally, if a Tropical Storm passes to the North of your position the winds will blow from the N to NW to SW If the storm center passes to the South of your position, the wind will blow from SE to E to S. This assumes that the storm's track is to the N or NW, but as evidenced by Klaus in '83 and Lenny in '99, storms do whatever they want. Buys Ballots' Law however, applies regardless of the storm's track.

There is a fly in the soup however, in that for everyone who applies some 'sea-sense' there will be someone with no-sense, and the truth be told, some boats are worth more 'dead' than alive so their owners take little precaution.

All preparations should be completed before conditions deteriorate beyond force 8 or force 9 winds. It is hard to walk in 50 knots of wind and hard to crawl in 80! Wear a full wet-suit and snorkel mask for warmth, protection, and ease of breathing if you must venture out. Keep your head down and hope no coconut or pieces of sheet metal are blowing in your direction If you are near mangroves, drive the bow as far into the trees as possible, the tide will probably rise, not fall. Better to be stuck in the trees than blown about with diminishing scope on your anchors. A friend of mine weathered Gilbert in the mangroves of Isla Mujeres in the Yucatan, with his wife and daughter aboard. After the storm they spent 3 months lowering the boat, but they survived and except for termites in his wooden mast, the boat was not damaged!

Remember that most casualties in Tropical Storms are from drowning or exposure and that we of the Maritime Community have perfect life saving and life sustaining systems inherent in our ships, if we are able to escape the almost certain destruction of lee shores, powerful ground seas and dragging fleets.

Good Luck to you this 'H' season, spill a bit of 'Jack-Iron' rum when you can-appease them, don't call them names (don't call them at all) please don't ignore them, but don't surrender too quickly either.

SAVING SOULS

Once again, the fishing community of the Grenadines, and that's just about everybody, has been worried about, or praying for three Union Island fisherman who went missing on Wed. 7 June. Fishing is, as I've stated before, a totally significant activity which supplies both protein and prestige. But what is the value of prestige if lives are lost? What then is the price of this kind of significance?

No one knows if the crew of "Peace and Love" (a 17' open boat) had a flare, any water or any single piece of life-saving gear aboard. Oars certainly, maybe three, but no whistle, probably no life jackets; this was just a short trip. Check the fishpots, maybe do a bit of tow-baiting. "Gonna make a broth". The boat was probably locally made, and knowing the skill level and the boats of the area, I'd say it was most likely sound. It was propelled by a 45 horsepower outboard motor; (troublesome at the best of times), it represented the only way to get back home. It also represented about 350 pounds of deadweight when in-operative. Very expensive ballast. The boat, built of wood would have reserve buoyancy, but at what point does someone begin considering the 'jettisoning' of what, next to his home, might be their most valuable possession? At what point do they surrender their 'ride home' for the long row, the long drift or the long wait?

I am often amazed at the amount of gear carried by some yachts—Water makers, washer/dryers, television, SSB, and navigation gear enough to make the bridge of the "Enterprise" appear dated. They almost all have internal diesel engine or engines, the full 'kit'. Yet a lot of these same vessels remain in harbor if the wind is over 20 knots and check for 'a window' to make a 25 mile trip. Fishermen here have neither the equipment nor the options. By the very nature of their work they go to sea almost daily, often under-equipped and any Windward Islands Seaman worth their salt know that the 'lee' side of 'here' can become the 'windward' side of 'there' very rapidly.

I have a 20 ton, locally built, and still engineless gaff cutter. It was built for just these same heavy conditions, but I have often taken a beating in my pursuit of an ocean fish or a windward mark. I do not carry a life raft aboard mermaid. I have instead a 12 foot locally built "two-bow" not unlike most of the small boat fleet here. I do however carry as well as oars; flares, orange smoke, life-jackets, a sea anchor, internal flotation and have a ditch kit which includes hats, shirts, a few cans of veggies in water, glucose wafers and a bag of chewing gum! All in a small yellow waterproof bag it's not much, but it's an edge. When all is said about our 'craft' and their differences we all have usually less than 2 inches of some hull material separating us from the sea, but if afloat and adrift, the depth of the sea pales in relation to it's breadth.

The Grenadian and St. Vincent Coast Guards conducted a joint search and were assisted by an aircraft from Puerto Rico. All looking for a 17 foot, red and white fishing boat with THREE SOULS ABOARD! Fishermen all, and paying one awful price to earn a living, feed their families and honor both their village and their nation. Herein I would like to make a modest proposal, costing nothing and perhaps saving a soul or two All yachts and ocean shipping, especially those carrying passengers for hire, are required by international law to carry distress and safety gear of the highest standards. This includes hand flares, rockets, smoke canisters, first aid kits, sea-anchors, dye markers and signal mirrors. At present, most of this equipment con-forms to SOLAS standards (The European standard of safety) and have a serviceable life of 6 years. The United States Coast Guard however has ruled that all such equipment must be re-placed every 3 years. Might not this 3 year "over-lap";be used, or taken advantage of by a progressive fisheries system, to insure that it's fishermen are at least minimally supplied with some safety gear and that their lives are thereby considered'significant'? Here is the 'crux' of the issue (as I see it, ahem). If you KNOW that a boat adrift has a flare or two for day (but better at night), or orange smoke for day (worthless at night), you will search more efficiently knowing that those in distress and possibly low in the water will almost always see or hear the searching ships or airplanes before being seen themselves.

There are many authorized "inspection and repackaging" facilities in the Eastern Caribbean and they are more than happy to give away—FREE, from their stockpile of "old" gear. Old, in most cases, being three years of age, still conveniently allowing three internationally accepted years of use prior to expiry date. Sea anchors do not expire. An "old" life-jacket or first-aid kit is better than no life-jacket or first aid kit. Expired perhaps…but still quite capable of saving a life! Yachtsmen in transit might also be willing to donate any 'expired' but still functional equipment to any fishery stations so they might be made available to the fleet, and the fishermen instructed in their use, but more importantly, the Island Governments, their fisheries and those agencies willing to supply equipment must be able to work in conjunction to protect those people who go to sea for a livelihood. As ever, it is Lives that are at stake here. Those that go to sea with their limitless ambition: yoked to their limited tools.

TO CATCH A FISH

Fishing is, has been, and probably always will be one of my favourite activities. As a child of the New England Coast my first idea or concern about the passage of time was a hazy concept defined by the 6 hour alternate high-low tidal cycle which changed my favourite fishing spots into favourite clam digging areas. W.I.-W.O. Water In-water Out, very dependable. An awareness heightened by the different smells of hi-lo water. I did not need to leave our beachside home, just take a deep breath and that sense of 'parfum natural' was awakened and I immediately knew whether to grab my 4-tyne clam fork or my 7 foot spinning pole with attached Mitchell 302 reel.

Now after over 30 years in the land of 18 inch tides and palm trees, my clam fork has rusted away with disuse but my fishing gear keeps being used on a pretty regular basis. I average over 500 miles and 13 days offshore a month, usually single-handed aboard my 20 ton engineless gaff cutter.

In October I boated over 400 pounds of pelagic fish and saw 3 species of whales not including smaller dolphins and assorted porpoises. I am doubly pleased to boat fish while anchored in a bay trolling from my 12 foot (150 pound) rowing dinghy. Within one mile of where I am currently anchored in Carriacou, from my dinghy, I have boated an amazing diversity of fishes including tarpon, bonefish, mackerel, bigeye and yellowfin tuna, crevalle jack, rainbow runner, pompano, palometto, yellowtail and mutton snappers, hinds, butterfish and assorted groupers! Incredible! Recently, both Jimmy Buffer and Mick Jagger were seen in the Harvey Vale mangroves fishing for tarpon. I heard that Jimmy even entered the spot on his airborne GPS! He apparently did not have much luck however and though he saw some of the worlds' biggest mullet he hooked up no tarpon. As for Mick, no one saw him come back out of the mangroves, so we are checking around to see if he made it back to Mustique OK. I thought I would check around to see if I couldn't discover why, with a local guide, Jimmy had had no luck. I approached my friend Ras Vaughn, who had taken Jimmy fishing, and Vaughn was a bit confused at first as to who I was speaking of. There are not many Parrotheads' among the local citizenry, so Jimmy's status as a rock-star went for naught.

"So how de fishenin' Vaughn?"

"Well John, we didn't catch a ting, de fella use dis funny pole wid a lot of swish-swish wrist and not even a piece of real bait. He was looking for a tampon fish."

"Hey, Vaughn, watch, dat is not a TAMPON, dat a TARPON."

"Oh, a tarpon. So John, what is a tarpon?"

"Dat is a 'Grand-ecaille' mon."

"Ohhhh!…a grand-ecaille, oh dat is it. Well, what he want he want dat for? Can't eat it…too many bones, and what de fish he call a 'bonefish'? Dere are lots of boney fish and dat tampon, or tarpon, is sure one of dem. So what is de bonefish?"

"Dat is de banan" Vaughn. They are great sport, especially on the fly rod used to catch them. Great Sport".

Now Vaughn didn't care too much about 'de sport', but he was beginning to realize that a leopard and it's spots often get confused. We chatted a bit more and Vaughn mentioned that he was surprised that a grown man would go through the trouble to catch a boney fish he was not going to eat and as a case in point he has even had people ask him if they might catch a 'snook' here! Well a snook in Carriacou is the 'Southern Sennet' a smaller cousin of the barracuda, scarcely 1 pound and maybe 16 inches long.

"He were lookin' for de 'Cr-Cru' Vaughn."

"Ohhhh! Well why he talking' all dis foreign name dem? Dat why de fella is so confused mon.", and so it goes. It is a good idea to learn a bit about local names, or better yet, bring a picture.

The 'Rainbow Runner' (a jack) is called a 'salmon' here. That has cause a lot of confusion, not unlike the first time a northerner hears a banana called a fig. People here know what a fig' is and it sure ain't the Persian fruit with all the seeds!

In the 1960s I operated a sport fishing boat out of Garrison Bright in Key West and it was rare to catch a rainbow runner. When you did it always turned heads; but here, I have seen a half-ton pick-up truck loaded with identical 6 pound fish! I have caught several myself, but it will never really be salmon to me, I know what salmon is

So if you are on holiday or cruising, take a bit of time and enjoy the fishing. As well as being a wonderful interlude in your schedule and pace, allowing you to get closer to the 'real world' West Indian style, you might just land a delicious dinner. The frosting on the cake being that. CIGUATERA is virtually unknown here in the Grenadines and just about everything, even the boney ones, are edible.

And Jimmy, if you read this, send that fishing 'pole to Vaughn. (you promised) They might not know a lot 'rock and roll' or what a parrot-head is, but they do know their fish and what a tampon is. And let us know if you've heard from Mick.

'SPICE' TRADE OR 'DRUG' TRADE?

As a "Nutmeggar", and not a very young one, I remember reading the slogans on American license plates. At that time the Connecticut plates did not say, "Constitution State" or "Live, Free or Die" as is the case in New Hampshire, (locally remembered as" Live Freeze and Die"). No Sir, Connecticut was the "Nutmeg State". They didn't grow any there, but you've got to understand, whaling was cold dangerous work and the trips were 5 years long! (Small wonder Ahab had a few loose screws.)

The SPICE TRADE!, now that not only sounds nice, it smells nice, and if you were lucky enough to have shipped a West Indian cook, it meant a good galley. Plus, it never, ever gets cold! Oh Bliss. the land where the butterstays melted the sun always shines and thought the pitch in the seams might get sticky one never suffered from frostbite! The land of cinnamon, vanilla,, annatto, pepper and that curse or blessing of humanity-opium and most famously here in Grenada and north in Connecticut—Nutmeg! NUTMEG (Mrystica fragrans)…a spice yes, a medecinal as well, so Valuable that the Dutch, in their attempts to monopolize the trade immersed The kernels in 'milk of lime' for 4 months to prevent germination!". Spice or medecine?

The rare and exotic became the "elixirs of life"—medicines, hence drugs. But when the spice became the medicine that became the drug the value increased significantly. Pharmacology slowly replaced a more once more common pharmacognsy and the priceless drug of pre 17th and 18th centuries medicine became the kitchen shelf jar of spice. Ethnobotany versus the world's economy and the world's fashions!

Just 25 years ago romantic images of the "Marlboro Man' were ubiquitous and it was considered fashionable to smoke. Bless or curse, Sir Walter Raleigh, but remember, he was ultimately be-headed. John Hawkins, Francis Drake and Martin Frobisher, were all privateers and within the realty of the time 'probably slavers', but more frequently they preyed upon the small, remote Spanish establishments and straggling Spanish ships at sea. Remember too, that to his most Catholic Magesty they were all the same-Heretics! As were those aboard the "Mayflower" at Plymouth, Mass. in 1620, all apt to be seized and burned on the spot. finit.

This was the time of the Inquisition. These superior English ships which so proved themselves in 1588 were already making a mark. Extracting a price from King Phillip and the Holy Roman Empire. Spanish cargo became English booty. The world clamoured for silver and gold but more importantly was rapidly getting addicted to spices. Sugar! Logwood! Lignum-Vitae, Pepper. The Spanish carried it all, they lost a bit to the 'pirates but had the last laugh and are probably laughing still for the best treasure, that rarest of spice, used as money by the Aztec that most royal of treasures CACAUTL///CACAO which Montezuma consumed daily as was his kingly privelage was chocolate. The ultimate luxury of the Spanish rich!

The Aztec called it cacao, old world pharmacists soon named it theobroma—"Food of the Gods". In it's raw form however the dried, crushed and cured cocoa rolled into little sticks or balls is in fact quite bitter and quite frankly—it looks like little turds-' Baby-poop', or 'caca'. Yeah, caca. (Vowels get dropped all the time) The food of the gods became known as baby turds. Our hardy English seafarers took these little sticks and balls and threw them into the sea and it was hundreds of years before Hershey, Cadbury or Toblerone establisted their own particular confectionaires, the income of which annually would rival that of the Spanish King in 1600! It's a funny world, and Montezuma, my heart goes out to you. Some idea of the number and nature of drug substances used in Medicine of 17th century may be obtained from records indicative of Charles the Second's treatment and death. The King had fallen while being shaved, probably a from a stroke and lost consciousness.

(He was bled a pint from the right arm and then cupped a pint of blood from his shoulder. This was followed by an enema containing antimony, sacred bitters, rock salt, mallow leaves, violets, beet roots, chamomile flowers, fennel seed, linseed, cinnamon, cardamom, saffron, cochineal and aloes. This was repeated in two hours, The Kings' head was shaved and a mustard poultice was applied. A sneezing powder of hellebore root and cowslip flowers was administerd to "strengthen the brain". A soothing drink of barley water, licorice, sweet almond, white wine, absinthe and anise was given as well as extracts of thistle, mint, rue and angelica. For external treatment a plaster of Burgundy pitch and pigeon dung was applied to his feet. To these medicaments was added melon seeds, manna, slippery elm, black cherry water, an extract of lime, lily-of-the-valley, peony, lavender and dissolved pearls. Later came gentian root, nutmeg, quinine and cloves.)

As a sort of grand summary to this pharmaceutical debauch a mixture of pearl julep and ammonia was forced down the Kings' throat. He expired despite all these brave attempts to rally him. So the spice trade was in retrospect the drug trade. a I guess not a lot has really changed. Ask any patient of modern medicine what it's like buying a new drug—expensive is what it is!

In 1503 when an Italian chap known only as Vespucci went in search of his own interpretation of the 'elixir of life', he first, and probably last, made non-violent contact with the people who used cacao beans as money. These "Indians" of the New World told him he had arrived at 'AMERRIQUE" (ref: Nat'l Geo.). That place which was the" meeting place of all the winds". Vespucci took it as a surname, and the new world was never named Columbia! 200 years later the sailors there on those flying fish runs to the spice isles took the time to become the best counterfeit nutmeg carvers in ethnobotanical history!

At one time almost one third of the nutmegs offloaded and shipped to New York or Boston were in fact carved from West Indian mahogany. And Connecticut Yankees became known as "Nutmeggars".

What new 'spice' of today will become the new wonder drug of tomorrow? What as yet un-classified tree or flower or seed will flavor our soft drinks or cure our cancer? What will it be named and what will it cost? What will it be worth? The Beautuful small island nation of Grenada is still truly the 'spice isle', but it is struggling to survive in the face of creeping globalization. It will however, perhaps be upon the shores of a small island nation such as this that maintains it's heritage of herbal traditions that a new" exotic", that a new spice might be re-discovered. A drug that cures and not just takes away the pain

GLOBAL WARMING RISING TIDES ME AND MY DOG

I must admit to being taken 'aback' by an article that recently appeared in Compass where in the writer has us put ice cubes in our glasses of water and be comforted by the fact that because the glass does not overflow we have nothing to fear in the event of melting polar ice. If all of the ice in the world were already floating the example would be apt. Most of the worlds' water (97.2%) is in the oceans, but when we consider the planet as a 'hydrosphere' we gain a better understanding of the balance and cycles of fresh water distribution between land, sea and atmosphere.

If we consider the annual circulation of the hydrosphere in "quadrillions of cubic meters" of fresh water, we find 13 units in the atmosphere, 200 in all of the lakes and rivers of the world, 7,000 in subsurface water and 26,000 in ice caps and glaciers. This means that frozen water on land is 130 times as common as all the water in all the lakes, rivers and clouds in the world.

One cycle of the Pleistocene," that geological era of time characterized by the rise and recession of continental ice sheets and the appearance of man" is approximately 90,000 years and 100,000 years ago or B.P., (Before Present) global sea levels were 8m or 25 feet higher than today. As the earth entered the last glacial period, the "Wisconsin" which peaked about 18,000 B.P. sea levels fell to 120 m or 370 feet lower than today. As recently as 7,000B.P. ocean levels in the region of the Antilles were 40m or 125 feet lower than today. St. Barths, St. Maarten and Anguilla were all one island and it would have been possible to walk from Grenada to Bequia! The coastal floodplains of Western Florida were vast grasslands with grazing Mammoth and Bison.

In the mid 70's an extinct land tortoise (Geochelone crassicutata) was found on a ledge now 29 meters under water and it had been killed by a fire hardened lance carbon dated at 12,030 B.P.

Water levels continued to rise until approximately 6,000-4,700 B.P. during the "Older Peron Submergence when the planets temperature averaged 2.5 degrees Celsius warmer than today and sea levels were 4 m or 13 feet higher than today. In July 0f 2001 the United Nations Conference on Global warming predicted just this same rise in temp over the next 100 tears!

It might be said that an knowledge of 'Hydraulics" parallels human development and has played no small role in his creation myths either. (The Biblical Flood, Gilgamesh, etc.) Recent findings in Egypt seem to show a rapid decline in the then dominant culture of the day when with the fall of world water levels at the end of the Peron Submergence the Nile Valley dried up and the Egyptian empire fell apart from mass starvation. With a lower water level on this side of the Atlantic an ambitious canoe people like the archaic "Wa'aroi" of the Orinoco basin could have easily migrated to Mainland Florida. Indeed the oldest watercraft in the Americas (6,000B.P.) was made of pine and found in Florida. These pre-historic dugouts were of the circum-carib type with platform ends; not the pointed types that the Polynesians and later Calusa were familiar with. In Venezuela, named after Venice for it's over water houses Indians lived in pile dwellings and used double canoes or "cayucos" which were in use in Florida at the time of European contact.

Ecological theory addresses universal issues such as evolution and "ideal vs. real" but oftimes considers people as intruders and thus tends to ignore pre-historic or contemporary influences of the planets dominant organism-Man. Historical-Ecology therefore provides at least a theoretical link between the evolution of culture and landscape. The most direct example of the connection between land-use and climate is through the change of surface "Albedo".

Albedo is the percentage of incident solar radiation reflected by a land or water surface. Evergreen forests have an albedo of 7-15%, plowed fields have an albedo of 10-15%, deserts of 25-30%, asphalt 8% and ice or snow 85-90%, but as surface ice melts it no longer reflects 85-90% of the suns' rays as light but absorbs heat which in turn melts more ice and so on. Remember too, that all human energy use ultimately ends up as residual heat, but the most 'anthropogenic' threat to the stability of climate are Carbon Dioxide emissions and releases of chemicals that deplete Stratospheric Ozone

The massive heat storage capacity of the oceans is one of the strongest stabilizing influences of the planets' climate and in the oceans' depths minute "phyto-plankton" annually fix 40 billion tons of carbon dioxide and release an equal amount of Oxygen. Fears of the effects of the devastation of Whale Pods upon the worlds oxygen supply induced the Governor and State legislature of Colorado to pass a condemnation of commercial whaling practices because, in the event of a disruption of the world" oxygen supply a city like Denver would suffer the most at 6000 feet.

Baleen whale individuals consume many tons of the larger species of carbon dioxide producing zooplankton and that plankton is now undergoing a classic population explosion. What will be the effect on the smaller oxygen producing phytoplankton? What effect will the changed color or reflectivity of the surface have on temperature and dissolved oxygen content? Just as we need living plants and stable "carbon-sinks' we might also need the whales to preserve the air we breathe.

The buried oil we now value as our economic life's' blood is a vast 'carbon-sink' as well but not all of prehistoric forests became oil. The perma-frost of circum-polar regions represents a vast amount of organic material safely frozen to a depth of hundreds or thousands of meters. In not the worst case scenario of the results of greenhouse warming and subsequent rising of the temperatures and tides the most rapid change is seen in the melting of polar ice, not much at first but when the perma-frost begins to thaw it begins its' potentially unstoppable transition from frozen carbon sink into more greenhouse gas. This is happening now.

For the first time in recorded history Thunderstorms are affecting the high latitudes of Canada. Strange new and never before seen species are migrating to the once frozen tundra, mosquitoes and a strange red-breasted bird—the ROBIN, for which there is no word in the languages of the Arctic. Now imagine a map with the North or South Pole as center, it is just as legitimate as a Mercator projection, but the only map to have in the Arctic. Imagine yourself in the center of that map watching the glaciers melt, seeing the perma-frost thaw…at the middle of climate change, with nowhere to go.

The Unted Nations prediction of tidal level rise of 4-6 meters by the close of this century would affect the Caribbean plenty and no amount of seawall will keep all that water away. Does anyone remember the decision the evacuate Port Elizabeth, Bequia in 1979 when volcanic activity threatened a 5 m tidal surge?

What if the tide came in and stayed?

CIGUATERA

Any angler or sailor worth their salt, know this is a poison to be taken seriously. Each year some 10,000 to 50,000 people fall victim to Ciguatera. First recorded in 1606, it wasn't until 1977 that its' transmission from a dinoflagellate was understood. The toxic Dinoflagellate "Gambierdiscus toxicus" grows on the surface of marine algae and is absorbed by herbivorous fish in temperate water. The toxic accumulates as it travels up the food chain through the predatory fish and eventually to man. The fish remain unharmed; there is no off odor, bad taste or discoloration. The toxin, being temperature stable, is not destroyed by cooking or freezing.

There are over 450 species of fish which can be ciguatoxic, but the larger tropical fish like the Barracuda, Grouper, Amberjack, Kingfish, Spanish mackerel and some Snappers are the most troublesome. Sporadic outbreak is typical of the toxins pattern. A reef may be contaminated one year and not the next while fishing grounds just a mile away may be perfectly safe. Disruption of the marine environment by construction projects and severe storms is probably a factor, but with a one to five year transfer up the food chain it is difficult if not impossible to pinpoint causal relationships.

I have been poisoned twice in the Caribbean. Once while crewing aboard the ketch Meroe of Kent, seven of us were poisoned after sharing a Spanish mackerel caught between Barbuda and St. Barths. We were enroute to sint Maarten for one of the Heineken Regattas, and to this day I blame our poor finish on the effects of the poisoning. All 7 persons aboard were alternately in the head or so sore in our arms and legs as to be unable to make efficient sail changes.

In 1974 I sat at a barbecue in the 'ghetto' of old St. Barths, adjacent to the yacht Club, enjoying the run, impromptu music and chatting with new friends the cruiser on my right took a piece of fish from the grill and I took one next to it and by morning he was dead and I was one sick puppy! I did not lose any teeth or hair but for 2 months was unable to hold a cup of tea without spilling it! Just recently my friend Ed Teja of M/V float Street wrote to me about an incident which occurred in Cumana, Venezuela and in fact requested that I write this article as a result of his experience there. It seems that the woman from whom he regularly bought fish took a Barracuda home to feed her family and three of her children died. On a similar note, anyone who has spent any time in the Virgin Island is well aware that giving someone a Kingfish caught on the south shore is not considered an act of kindness.

Anyone eating a ciguatoxic fish suffers a bizarre blend of symptoms; nausea, vomiting, blurred vision and a reversal of the hot/cold sensations. The first clinical description of the syndrome was that of the Portuguese biologist Don Antonio Parra, who authored a volume published in Havana in 1787. It was in this account that the spelling of the name of the disease was 'siguatera' and the original description of the disease from this book is as follows:

In the exposition of the fishes I have talked about, I have said that some cannot be eaten because they are "Siguatos' and some others are suspicioned because they carry with them the poison. So that the reader will become acquainted with the nature of Siguatera I will give a short description; although this is probably more appropriate for physicians, since they come in contact every day with patients which have the affliction. You feel the effects of the poison almost immediately after you have eaten it. The initial symptoms are the following: your color becomes pale, your features moribund, your eyes dull, you suffer intense pain in your joints, bones, and a lack of appetite, increase tactile sensation, purging, vomiting and an intense itching all over the body, skin blemishes, ulceration, prostration and many other symptoms may be present. I speak from personal experience, because on 15 March 1786, twenty-two of us ate a Cubera, and we all developed those symptoms to a greater or lesser extent. My family became so debilitated that it was necessary for us to obtain some assistance the following day. All were prostrated, but each one was suffering various types of discomfort, although the most common type of difficulty was the extreme exhaustion accompanied by pain. I took lemonade from which I received some relief. I had extreme difficulty in breathing which caused great pain and a feeling of suffocation. My tongue became rough and I developed a sour taste in my mouth."

In the 19th century the principle work on Ciguatera was that of the Cuban ichthyogist Felipe Poe y Alloy and in this work he noted that there had been enacted an ordinance prohibiting the sale of any suspected fish of over 3 pounds. Each year there are cases reported in Hawaii, Japan, the East Indies and the Caribbean. Dr. Bruce Halstead and his colleagues report a mortality rate of from 7 to 12 per cent. Complete recovery sometimes taken many months or years. Mankind has been aware of the illness for over 6,000 years but modern medical science has yet to completely unravel the mystery of its origin or to prevent its annual fatal occurrence. The good news is that Dr. Yoshitsuga Hokama at the University of Hawaii is on the brink of changing all of that. Hokama has developed a simple stick-test' which has established a perfect track record since 1979 for detecting ciguatoxic fish. Hokamas' approach is to test a specific fishing ground and if less than 5-10% of a catch is toxic, the area is considered safe. Fortunately for us in the southern Caribbean, the Grenadines fall within this 'safe' limit. However, for fishermen whose catch of the day is a 60# grouper that has the potential to poison a crowd, individual testing is still worth it. (Note yellow fin grouper is 'Mycteroperca venonosa'!). Ciguatera is no longer a problem confined to the tropics. With tourism and worldwide exports on the rise, it is finding its way onto the 'mainland' in increasing numbers.

TO AVOID CIGUATERA: Watch and listen for outbreaks in waters you will be cruising. Avoid reef fish entirely where there have been recent cases. Pelagic fishes like marlin, dorado or tuna have not been known to cause outbreaks. Do not eat organs from reef fish (brain, spinal cord, intestines, bones, skin, gonads, roe or liver), as the toxic is up to 100 times more concentrated than in muscle tissue. Make it a point to know what fish you are eating. Almost any whole fish small enough to fit on your plate is probably ok. If affected avoid reef fish entirely for at least 3 months. Multiple poisonings increase sensitivity to the toxin. Alcoholic beverages, nut and seed products should be avoided during the illness.

My Merck manual advises that unless violent vomiting or diarrhoea has occurred, or symptoms appeared several hours after food was ingested, efforts should be made to remove the poison by gastric lavage. A saline cathartic of sodium sulphate (15 to 30GM) orally in water may be required. "Mannitol is believed to abbreviate if not abate the clinical sequence of Ciguatera Poisoning, Preliminary evidence suggests that the earlier a victim is diagnosed and treated the more likely the success with mannitol". (Donna G Blythe MD).

Standard dosage: is one (1) gram of mannitol per kilo of body weight. Mannitol injection 25% U.S.P. is available from most pharmacies in 50cc bottle (each containing 12.5 grams of mannitol). If we assume the average person to weigh 75 kilos we will require 6 bottles to have 75 grams of mannitol. At 50 cc each this would be 300cc. To this we add the remaining quantity (700cc) to form a liter (1000cc) of either 5% dextrose and water (D5W) or 9% sodium chloride (.9NaCI). This solution is then infused at a rate of 250-350cc per hour for a total procedure time of 3-4 hours. Mannitol should not be used by patients suffering cardiac pulmonary edema

FOR ENERGENCY ADVICE CONTACT: THE CIGUATERA HOT LINE (305) 361-4619 or (305) 661-0774.

MAY HOPE MASTER MY FEAR

It has been about 15 years since my good friend and fellow single hander, French Pete, of the 45 foot Carriacou sloop 'Gypsy Girl' was found stabbed to death aboard his boat in a secluded Colombian anchorage and almost 15 years ago the 63 foot Bequia schooner 'Water Pearl' found herself upon the windward shore of Panama with a broken back. Her bones lie there still. And only 6 months ago since another friend of mine was run down by a Venezuelan ferryboat while enroute to Grenada where we were to rendezvous and sail together as two singlehanded ships to the Virgin Islands. Lon Matlock has had to put his travel plans on hold. While under sail, close-hauled, on the starboard tack, he was overtaken and "sideswipped".

The 'Conferry' passed so close as to tear down his mast, tear off his bowsprit and crack the hull of his Westsail 32, 'Liberation'. Lon sits in Margarita waiting to see if he will be compensated by the ferry company which dis-claims all responsibility. Maybe they have conveniently forgotton that according to Rule 13 of the International Collision Regulations, "The overtaking vessel is always burdened and must keep out of the way of the vessel being overtaken and that this applies regardless of the conditions or the characteristics of the vessels involved." But there are thousands of people in the streets of Venezuela calling President Chavez and he doesn't seem to hear them so why should he hear a 72 year old singlehanded American sailor? Likewise, who heard French Petes' cry for help as he bled to death in his berth? Bad time-Bad place. As for the 'Water Pearl'; President Noriegas' Panama in the spring of 1988 was a bad place to shipwreck. The country was under a complete embargo and the American military were effecting a "regime change". Even if the boat had not been doomed by the damage done in the grounding, no commercial help was available. A team of Navy SEALS loaned the use of a few Navy 'Mike" boats (LCM), but to no avail. I understand that the wreck was stripped and the hull later used for 'counter-insurgency' and 'anti-terrorist' training

In all of these cases there is a certain blending of the variables of chance, luck, complacency and foolishness, but equally common is that that they all occured along the coasts of Caribbean territories that have gone through violent political and economic change these past few decades and not very frequently for the better. Sailors are however often among the first of travellers to visit and linger. This is often adventuresome, no less and sometimes more of an attraction and maybe even, make that usually, less expensive than visiting the main-line yachtsmans' resorts. While cruising the Venezuelan coast in the mid 70's aboard an engineless trimaran, I more than once escaped what I considered malicious intent by cracking sheets and reaching into the north at 14 knots.

Many years later aboard my slower but sea-kindlier gaff cutter I must admit to having been boarded in, Puerto Rico, St. Thomas, Martinique, Dominica, Grenada, Jamaica, Honduras, Mexico and Florida by young uniformed men pointing automatic weapons at me. On each of these occasions, after the first spasm of shock and fear, then acceptance and ultimate surrender to 'authority', I wished that I had just stayed away, but I guess that's the price a cruiser pays when he leaves the beaten track and returns again. When a large part of the eastern Caribbean has been turned into a theme park with 'Bareboat' as season ticket, it is no wonder that a certain minority of sailors want to, in the words of Capt. Kirk, "Go where no one has gone before". With rising sea levels there may soon be more anchorages but there are already to many boats and twice as many people in the world as when I started cruising in the 60's. The opportunity of going "yachting" therefore doesn't always lead us away but sets us more in the midst. We are more easily involved and consequently more affected by our inter-actions. Unlike the Disney theme park, 'Pirates of the Caribbean', where tourists play no active role but only observe, cruising sailors take a very active role in this dance of freedom

There aren't as many 'secluded' spots anymore. With increased security comes the crowd, and it is not so much the GPS that has changed the cruising scene, it is all those diesel engines and electric windlasses. Was a time when you couldn't always just 'up' your hook and go, so you gave more thought as to where to 'down' it.

The dance floor is getting crowded and that is, for some, reason to celebrate, but there will always be those who will stray from the cruising guide paths so finely drawn. We might be advised to remember though that even if our charts are true our conceptions often prove false. The world changes, it grows as the ocean seems to shrink, and I acknowledge this but 'Gypsy Girl' and Pete are gone, 'Water pearl' is gone and a 72 year old singlehander was run down and then forgotten. So much for the Freedom of the Sea and the Rules of the Road. I should not be so quick to judge. For several hundred years wasn't it 'Freedom of the Sea' that divided nations, fomented wars and took countless lives here in the Caribbean? For the past 500 years didn't religions, nations, Kings, guilds, pirates and traders intentionally set up trade barriers or embargoes against the free passage of ships or individuals with whom there were no 'trade agreements'? No one sticks their neck out and talks about 'right of passage', might as well shout 'save the whales or maybe even cry'wolf'. No one is listening. It is now and always was a trade issue, a question of money, of profit, of cash flow. A yacht by definition is not engaged in trade, but the legacy viewing everything in terms of its 'cash value' has sadly left the cruiser as appearing involved in an exercise of displaying ostententatious wealth. If we run aground our ships represent so much 'flotsam and jetsam' and just as often plain 'booty' to strangers who do not understand our lives and would do us harm. We pay our taxes to enter and very often pay some heavy dues to leave…very few carry as much 'in' and so little 'out' as the crew of a shipwrecked or pirated vessel.

I am reminded of and take strength from Capt. Joshua Slocum who having crossed the equator and enroute to home in 1898 first heard of the Spanish-American War then raging. Asked in flag hoist by the US Battleship OREGON if he had seen any 'enemy' shipping, Josh hoisted a reply of 'no', and then as an afterthought and with a Yankee chuckle he hoisted another signal which read, "Let us keep together for mutual protection". Capt. Clark of the OREGON did not deem this necessary, but he did dip his ships' ensign Three times to the 'Spray'. That night Capt. Slocum, "pondered long over the probability of a war risk coming upon the "Spray"…But, A STRONG HOPE MAS-TERED MY FEARS.' Happy is the helmsman of a sailing ship who is content with his lot.

AFTERWORD

I once had a teacher who said that every person views their life through their own private window: that every window has its own unique view, and therefore we all view reality in our own particular way. Captain John Smith is a Caribbean character, vagabond, roustabout, sailor, jack-of-all trades, ecologist, survivor, writer and poet, who is taking full advantage of the view through his own personal porthole. 'This collection' gives us a chance to take a peek through that porthole. It is quite an interesting view.

What we see is a man who is fully, without hesitation, living life to it's fullest. It is encouraging to see that there are still people out there who will not trade their philosophy or convictions for time-share anywhere. The stock market sometimes dives and might go to the moon tomorrow. All that wouldn't mean diddly squat to the skipper of this 'ol Mermaid, he just caught a twenty five pound dorado. He may not be able to afford to blow a thousand bucks at the casino, but he has food for a week.

In the world today it is not easy to stay true to one's convictions. To be jaded and complacent is simple. Perhaps we can learn something here. It is about time. As John says, "We are all endangered species."

—Chris Bowman, Bicton, Australia.

0-595-26361-5

CPSIA information can be obtained at www.ICGtesting.com
Printed in the USA
BVOW020740081011

273099BV00002B/111/A